The Humor, the Horror, and the Heart of the Badge

The Life and Times of an Itinerant Police Officer

D. Chris Schultz

The Humor, the Horror, and the Heart of the Badge
ISBN: Softcover 978-1-960326-05-8
Copyright 2023 by D. Chris Schultz

All rights reserved. No part of this book may be reproduced or transmitted in any form or by any means, electronic or mechanical, including photocopying, recording, or by any information storage and retrieval system, without permission in writing from the publisher.

Scripture quotations are from the King James 1611 Authorized Version of the Holy Bible.

Photographs of all six police officers featured in chapter thirteen are used with permission of the Officer Down Memorial page. The photograph of Ms. Wang is used with permission of her husband Carl Ibsen.

Parson's Porch Books is an imprint of Parson's Porch & Company (PP&C) in Cleveland, Tennessee. PP&C is a self-funded charity which earns money by publishing books of noted authors, representing all genres. Its face and voice is **David Russell Tullock** (dtullock@parsonsporch.com).

Parson's Porch & Company *turns books into bread & milk* by sharing its profits with the poor.

www.parsonsporch.com

The Humor, the Horror, and the Heart of the Badge

The Life and Times of an Itinerant Police Officer

Contents

Dedication 7
Foreword 9
Author's Preface 11
CHAPTER ONE 13
   The Early Years of a Future Public Servant: Captain Crunch, Bad Breaks, and Bicycle Follies
CHAPTER TWO 25
   Behind Every Good Man Is a Good Woman, Even If He Is Directionally Challenged
CHAPTER THREE 35
   Not Only the Marines Have Uncle Sam's Misguided Children
CHAPTER FOUR 49
   High-Test Patterson, the Listerine Man, and Moon Mullins
CHAPTER FIVE 72
   Mayberry Is Not in Montana!
CHAPTER SIX 81
   My Dream Come True? Bombs, Bullets and Boondoggles
CHAPTER SEVEN 117
   Every Cop's Worst Nightmare
CHAPTER EIGHT 142
   Where Do I Go from Here? A Second Chance from "Second Chance"
CHAPTER NINE 152
   Starting Over and Fast Becoming the World's Oldest Rookie
CHAPTER TEN 159
   On The Road Again, Chasing Taillights and Encountering Tragedy
CHAPTER ELEVEN 170
   The Golden Years: The Rookie Rides Again
CHAPTER TWELVE 185
   The Rookie Rides Off into the Sunset, or Does He?
CHAPTER THIRTEEN 201
   Remembering the Fallen: Gone, Yet Not Forgotten
EPILOGUE 211

Dedication

To my beautiful wife Carole and my wonderful kids and kids-in-law who inspired and encouraged me to write this memoir, I dedicate this book. I love all of you with all my heart. You have given me more than I ever deserved through your love and support throughout my life and career. May that love continue long after I am gone, and may you always respect and support my brothers and sisters of the Thin Blue Line.

May all of my fellow officers with whom I had the privilege to work during my career please know that a part of you lives on through these pages, for I was honored to work with such courageous men and women as you.

I want to thank Missoula retired County Sheriff Carl Ibsen and retired Police Chief Doug Chase of the Missoula Police Department, as well as my sister Connie Reynolds and our daughter Kristi Mitchell who spent hours painstakingly editing and correcting my many grammatical errors. English was not one of my strong subjects. I especially want to thank my editor Charles Davidson who believed in this project and whose efforts have made this a far better read than I could have accomplished on my own. His wisdom and Christian fellowship during this project have made me a better writer and I will be forever in his debt. Thanks also to his lovely wife Georganne who was so gracious to lend me her husband.

Foreword

The Humor, the Horror, and the Heart of the Badge is a must read for all who are interested in gaining an inside look at the world, the life, and the mind of cops. Virtually anyone will find this memoir engaging, sometimes shocking and sad, and always informative. It provides persons who are not in the law enforcement profession a glance into the everyday realities of those whose calling is to be a police officer. Those who belong to the profession, including myself with over forty-two years behind the badge, will discover that Chris Schultz's story triggers a myriad of vivid memories that are happy and even funny, yet at other times horrific and tearful.

Chris opens himself up to you, the reader, as he paints the mural of his life as a cop. He gives you glimpses into events that made national news, and you will meet officers he knew who were at their epicenter. Through it all he shows that cops are people like everyone else, yet with a high calling that assumes far higher risk than many occupations.

Chris weaves his deep Christian faith into the narrative, demonstrating how the guidance and protection of God has kept him alive and healthy, and his family safe and intact through the challenging ups and downs that law enforcement families experience.

Throughout our long personal association, Chris helped me renew and strengthen my own faith, which had taken a beating through the years. Having worked with Chris for such a long time, I have known him well and trust him with my life. I have had the privilege and honor of calling Chris my friend and my brother of the badge.

I enthusiastically commend Chris's story to you. You won't be disappointed. C. C. Ibsen (Badge 146, Missoula Police Department, 1972–1993, Patrol, Detective, Motors, Retired as Sergeant; Badge 446, Missoula County Sheriff's Office, 1993–2011, Patrol, Captain of Patrol; Badge 41, Missoula County Sheriff's Office 2011–2014, Retired as Sheriff)

As I read "The Humor, The Horror and the Heart of the Badge" I almost felt like there should have been an addendum to the title of the book, which could have read "…Honored by our Great God". God honors faithfulness and also protects those of us who sometimes get derailed Chris Schultz has done a magnificent job of using words to remind us that if we will submit to His will for our lives, He will put the right people in our path (even "Listerine Man"). He will also put us in the right state, town and community and He will even place us under his wing when shots are fired…at us…and actually hit us?

This book is a tremendous blessing to any young person who is considering a career, not just to make a living, but too SERVE people and SERVE our Great Savior, The Lord Jesus Christ.

David Jeffers Th.M.
Pastor, Bible Baptist Church
Seymour, TN

Author's Preface

Nearly every little boy and many a little girl want to become a police officer at one time or another. That age-old game of cops and robbers has been played by children all over the country. The flashing red and blue lights of patrol cars with sirens blaring, on their way in response to an emergency, draws a certain fascination and wonder. The uniform and all of the accessories, including the weapon holstered to the police officer's side, induce awe from some, and fear from others.

Throughout my career I performed many kiddie talks to pre-school, Kindergarten, and younger-age classes, introducing children to the subject of law enforcement. While I also gave similar talks to junior and senior high school convocations, civic organizations, and senior citizen groups, I enjoyed the young children the most. You might ask why?

Having raised four children of my own, I realized how impressionable children are and how important it is to set a good example for them. But more importantly I wanted to let children know that police officers are approachable persons to whom they can come when they are in need of help. For cops are available in their communities to protect them.

Giving children the opportunity to see us police officers as trustworthy human beings is crucial to establishing future relationships with them as adults. We may never actually see the fruits of our labors first hand, but I like to think that the many kids who grow up to become police officers are a testimony to the fact that our efforts are not in vain.

In a time when a multitude of how-to books, self-help articles, and media platforms push various agendas, this memoir is my way, from an insider's perspective, of giving people a glimpse of what it means to be a cop.

My passion in life has been law enforcement. I loved the job during good times and downright bad times. I couldn't imagine doing anything else with the life God gave me.

To those of you who pick up this book to find out what could possibly be in its pages, I trust it will bring a smile to your face along with some laughter, and perhaps a tear or two to your eyes as you live vicariously through the stories that in one way or another answer your questions as to what a police officer's day on the streets of our cities is all about.

To you veteran police officers, I trust that you will understand just how important your contributions are to your communities. If I stir up memories both good and bad, my desire is that you employ those memories as a way to heal and put your personal demons behind you. You might even laugh at yourself as you laugh at me and the exploits of other officers who took to heart their responsibilities with the same seriousness with which you do.

To you, the rookie, staring at a blank page as you begin your career, you may discover that your experiences turn out to be quite similar to mine, although they will surely be your own for having been different from mine. You have chosen a noble profession. Never forget this. It is up to you to pick up the burdens that we who are retired have left behind, some having bled and others died when those burdens were far more than trivial and no less than hard.

Do your duty to the best of your ability, and never ever tarnish the badge of authority entrusted to your integrity and courage. No matter what life may throw your way, you have a tradition to uphold that stands at the foot of the graves of all of your fellow brothers and sisters in blue who have made the ultimate human sacrifice.

To you the citizen curious enough to read this book, I pray that by the time you finish it you will have better understood those officers who currently serve your community, and that you will see their efforts in a more human light than by the shadows of darkness that are cast by the appalling deeds of a few of them.

If you find yourself as a victim of a crime, or even in a situation that warrants an arrest or citation, realize that the officer standing before you is doing the job that is required for your sake and that of the larger community. Cooperate, even if you feel wronged. For the place to argue is not the street but in the courtroom. Realize that, just as is the case with you, officers have bad days and good days and want to go home to their families at the end of a day's or night's shift.

So, accompany me now, if you will, on the journey that God led me to take as one police officer responding to the many radio calls and dispatches that you will find within these pages as you immerse yourself in *The Humor, the Horror, and the Heart of the Badge*.

D. Chris Schultz

CHAPTER ONE

The Early Years of a Future Public Servant: Captain Crunch, Bad Breaks, and Bicycle Follies

Every story has a beginning and an ending. For me, my world debut took place on a cold January day in 1959, within a small hospital in Whitefish, Montana, thanks to Donald Lee and Ila Jean Abney Schultz, the latter better known as Billie.

I was the third child in line behind my sister Connie and brother Brian. My dad had been born in Enid, Oklahoma, but was raised primarily in Montana near the small community of Shawmut, where his father and mother homesteaded early in the twentieth century. There he enjoyed a life of hunting and fishing in his beloved Snowy Mountains. He was educated in a one room schoolhouse that allowed him to skip a grade because he did the work of two years in one. He graduated from Shawmut High School before going to work with his dad and brothers as a carpenter on the Winnecook ranch. In 1944. During World War II, he enlisted in the United States Navy.

At the time of his enlistment, the country was building its ranks for war against the Japanese in the Pacific. While every other recruit was destined for the Marine Corps, Army and Navy recruits alternated among them as they stood in line.13 Consequently, the recruits standing on either side of Dad were chosen for the Marines. Neither made it home alive from the war. Why God chose to spare my father from the same fate, I don't know. Call it providence or call it fate, we will not know this side of Heaven. I guess I could say that God was looking out for Dad and, by proxy, me, long before I was so much as a glint in Dad's eye. He served stateside until the war's end, training primarily with the fire-control weapons systems aboard ships. He was slated to take one of the last ships sailing for the Pacific from New York. But as fate would have it, the car in which he was riding, along with one of the ship's executive officers, got lost on the way to the pier. They arrived moments after the ship sailed. The Navy decided to reassign rather than transport them to their ship.

One of Dad's fondest memories from New York was sliding down the banister of the Waldorf Astoria Hotel, a tradition frowned upon by the hotel administration yet nevertheless practiced by many a service member. His next training assignment was in Washington, DC, close to where I would be stationed many years later in the service. He also undertook training stints in Florida and California. On one occasion while on leave, he hitchhiked across the country from Washington, DC, to Montana and back, all within in a week's time. He did not have to pay for a single meal along the way and hardly walked at all. World War II servicemen in uniform invariably relied upon strangers to stop and give them a ride. In Dad's case, they not only provided a ride but also paid for his meals.

Dad's best friend in the service was a gentleman by the name of Connie Shubach from Detroit, Michigan. He and Dad were determined to name their firstborns after one another in honor of their friendship. As men, naturally they assumed they would have boys, but both were blessed with girls as their firsts. Within our family the firstborn was my sister Connie, while Connie Shubach's own firstborn was to be a girl named Donna. It seems that God possesses a sense of humor about our desire to influence the course of life, including, among other things, the fickleness of the human birth order. How else to explain the appearance of the duck-billed platypus?

Many people, if thinking of God's involvement at all, may believe God to be a cosmic killjoy. But then, could anything be further from the truth? As Jesus said, "Even the very hairs of your head are all numbered. Fear not therefore: ye are of more value than many sparrows" (Luke 12:7).

So if God is attentive to the number of hairs on our heads, then surely God values us beyond just what's atop our heads, including those of us who have little or nothing up there to show.

* * *

After being discharged from the service, Dad returned to Montana, where he met and married my mom, Ila Jean Abney.

Accompanied by his best friend, Chet Skilbred, who had served in the South Pacific, the two of them wound up returning home on the same bus. At the very moment that they stepped off of it and into Harlowton, Montana, my mom and her sister Alice happened to be standing there, gazing through an apartment window.

As the story goes, each turned to the other and said, "We should marry those good-looking guys." The rest is history. My parents said their wedding vows in a small ceremony with my Uncle Chet and Aunt Alice in attendance, already having married a short time before. Mom and Dad spent their honeymoon, accompanied by Chet and Alice, on the backs of Harley Davidson motorcycles. Mom said she was not fond of the memory since she nearly froze to death. The December winter in Montana is unforgiving, especially for open-air cyclers, whether honeymooning or not.

Mom had grown up in Harlowton, just west of Shawmut. I always admired my dad for marrying her, because he knew that eventually she would likely become an invalid. Mom had been one of the first in the United States to be diagnosed with childhood rheumatoid arthritis. She spent the bulk of those early years in and out of hospitals, often with stays lasting months at a time. Dad's love for her proved far greater than any disease could diminish.

Together they traveled all over Montana while Dad worked as a carpenter. My earliest memory is of an old red pedal car in Wolf Point, Montana. At some point during our stay there, I fell down at one of my dad's job sites and cut my wrist on a nail. I still bear the scar today. Dad carried me home and doctored me up. I must have been about two years old at the time.

I was approximately that age when we moved to Missoula, Montana, and for the next four-plus years lived in the Target Range Trailer Court, where one of my neighbors, Mark Rosenbaum, became a lifelong friend. Both of us being from families of veterans, we easily took to watching the wild west television programs of Gene Autry, Roy Rogers, John Wayne, and Audie Murphy, and playing cowboys and Indians as we refought battles of the Civil War and World War II in our imaginations.

At any early age, I seemed to sense deep down that I was destined to join the military, or at least the cavalry. When I learned that the horse cavalry no longer existed, I was sorely disappointed. Mark Rosenbaum, always wanting to be a cowboy, followed his dreams. He now owns a ranch in Casper, Wyoming. For some years we remained at odds with one another due to my Christian faith and my stand for Jesus as Lord. Yet years later, Mark also came to faith in Christ. Now we are not only friends but also brothers in Christ. Eventually I would join the Army and become a military policeman.

After fulfilling enlisted active duty in the Army, I enlisted in the National Guard where I first served in the infantry and then as an armored cavalryman before finally separating from the National Guard.

While in the first grade, I entered a local IGA contest promoting the debut of Captain Crunch cereal and won a brand-new Western Flyer bicycle that was too big for me to ride at the time. For three years it sat idle, waiting for me to catch up to the task.

* * *

During our last year in the trailer court, Dad built a house for us on Missoula's Mount Avenue in order to accommodate Mom's disability. Shortly before moving to our new home in 1966, Mom surprised us with the birth of twin baby brothers. She had barely been wheeled out of the delivery room, having given birth to Kenny, when she said to the doctor that she believed she was not quite through yet. Sure enough, much to the shock of both of my parents, Keith was born eleven and a half minutes later.

I still recall Dad's scrambling to find another high chair and various other items that would be needed once the twins came home. The surprise of twins turned out to be a blessing in disguise. Mom's arthritis had been getting worse for years. But for the necessity of caring for two little monsters, she probably would have wound up in a wheel chair. I can attest to that fact from having lived with them. Though they were as cute as buttons, by the time they reached age four, they became known to the next-door neighbor as those "d**n twins."

On one occasion Mom momentarily lost her mind, or so it seemed, by allowing the twins to tie her up with a rope while they pretended to be cowboys. She figured she would take the part of the proverbial damsel in distress tied to the railroad tracks, to be rescued by her two gallant heroes. But not so. Given her arthritis, she couldn't untie herself and had to go next door for rescue by a neighbor. When she returned home, unencumbered by her bonds, the twins had locked the door, and refused to let her in. They proceeded to use the kitchen drawers as step stools to reach the countertop from which they emptied the contents of the cabinets. Fortunately, in time, they grew to become respectable citizens, or so they said. Being Cub Scouts, everyone knew they would never lie!

We moved into our new home while I was a second grader. What a sizable change it was, after having lived in a forty-foot trailer, to find ourselves in what seemed like a four-bedroom mansion. We all thought we had died and gone to heaven, except for my sister

Connie who felt deprived for not having lived but a short time in her spacious new bedroom. For, soon after we moved in, she married Dick Reynolds. We loved Dick and figured she'd be all right with someone else to look up to besides Brian and me. I spent many a night at Connie's and Dick's house throughout my teen years, and likely stayed out of considerable trouble because of them.

Although not raised by Christians, I was reared in a home where I was taught about honor, respect, and discipline. My parents were children of the Great Depression, growing up on homesteads. They were of the generation where a handshake was your word and your word was your bond. I got my fair share of spankings at the end of a leather belt when I was younger, and I recall that soap for washing out the mouth was not listed on the daily breakfast, lunch, and dinners menus. But I was never abused. Neither did I feel so. I knew for certain that my mom and dad loved me.

In later years, I endured my fair share of groundings, and the one thing I learned was that I did not want to disappoint my dad. He was my hero. He was my chief example as to how a man should live and work. Was he perfect? No. Was he human? Yes. My siblings and I had chores to do that we were expected to complete. My dad was not above cleaning the house, washing the dishes, or doing the laundry. He helped Mom with these tasks because he loved her and understood her limitations due to the arthritis. Even during subsequent years when their marriage was not at its best, he stood by her. His example taught us the importance of standing by one another, no matter what.

Mom was also a powerful example. She did not experience a single pain-free day in her life. Occasionally, one of us found her crying alone in pain, but she seldom complained. She pushed herself to remain as mobile as possible until the end of her days.

* * *

As I think about my relationship to my parents, a verse from the Gospel of John remained instrumental to their wellbeing and mine: "For God so loved the world, that he gave his only begotten son, that whosoever believeth in Him should not perish, but have everlasting life" (John 3:16).

My dad received Christ into his life in 1990. He came to realize that the Gospel's phrase, "whosoever believeth," pointed to him. As good a man as he was—many testified to the fact—he still needed a personal relationship with the Lord. Dad's salvation was one of the greatest answers to prayer I have ever received.

I was the first in my family to accept Christ into my life. Subsequently, for years, I prayed for Mom, Dad, and my siblings to accept Him as well—a subject to which we will return later. After Dad opened himself to Christ, a distinct change marked his life.

My mom had always said that she knew the Lord, but on the day that my dad passed away she realized that she needed Christ more than ever. Our pastor led her to Christ, which was yet another great answer to prayer.

To this day, I catch myself wanting Dad's advice, and have even found myself starting to dial his number a time or two. Likewise, I miss my mom's infectious, dry sense of humor.

I attended Target Range Elementary School for the entire eight years of grade school. While the experience was rich for being filled with various activities that included riding my bike, playing with friends, and accomplishing my school work, my friend Mark moved away for a while, as a result of which I felt lost without him. Thankfully, a few years later his family returned and our friendship flourished.

At the age of eight, I survived my first brush with death when a car sideswiped me while pedaling my bicycle home from school. I was a bit bruised, but more scared than hurt. Even though it would be some years before I recognized my need for Christ in my life, in hindsight I believe that God was looking out for me. The bicycle was bent up a bit, but Dad turned it back into shape in no time. With four boys growing up in his house, the incident should have been an omen for him. My mishap only foreshadowed the numerous vehicles he would repair over the years.

At the time, Missoula was a great place to grow up. For the most part it was a fairly conservative place, so far as college towns go, while being primarily a lumber and cow town. Unfortunately Missoula no longer has the small town atmosphere it once had. As the city has grown, so has the crime rate and the inclination to move away from traditional family values, as in many of the towns I knew in my childhood. Still, Missoula will always hold a place in my heart, as do my dear friends who dwell there. Some of my finest partners in law enforcement live there. I miss its people, the Rockies, and its wildlife, even though I don't miss its snowstorms. I suppose that I have turned into one of those proverbial human "snow birds," except for the fact that, once I decided to "fly" south for the winter, I stayed put and did not return to Missoula.

During those early elementary school years, however, I did the unthinkable. I literally broke my neck one day by jumping up and down on my bed, only to land on the headboard that Dad had made for it. My neck remained quite sore for several months until the pain gradually subsided. At the time, I said nothing to my parents for fear of getting into trouble. I kept my mouth shut until my teen years when I began to experience migraine headaches. My mother eventually took me to a doctor who, needless to say, took x-rays. The first thing she asked my mom was, "When did your son break his neck?"

Mom was thoroughly shocked, and replied, "He never has." Instantly, upon recalling my youthful frolicking upon the bed and tumbling into the headboard, I confessed my miscreant behavior to my mother, to which the doctor exclaimed, "You're lucky you're not paralyzed or worse." The break to my neck should have killed me.

The doctor noted that spinal bone growth had healed the fracture. The only long-term damage I experienced was a shortened neck. At the time, this seemed of little concern to me. But upon entering the military service, I looked altogether horrid in a steel pot helmet. With the appearance of my abbreviated neck I became known to my fellow trainees as Head-and-Shoulders Schultz. Thus concluded another scrape with the Grim Reaper, which on my part prompted no immediate thought of committing my life to God. Nonetheless, God remained committed to me, watching over me all the while.

Upon completing elementary school, I attended Hellgate High School in downtown Missoula. There I became active in Key Club and enjoyed the fellowship of other students as well as involvement in community service projects. As a young teenager, my cousins Brad and Kevin Schultz, along with my Uncle Herman and Aunt Marilyn Schultz, invited me to participate in some fellowship gatherings of Christians. It was then for the first time that I heard a clear presentation of the gospel and began to comprehend the fact that I was a sinner.

The Bible, God's Word revealed to us, states: "For all have sinned and come short of the glory of God" (Rom 3:23). Furthermore, "The wages of sin is death, but the gift of God is eternal life through Jesus Christ our Lord" (6:23).

From those words of St. Paul's letter to the Christians at Rome, I realized that Christ had died for me. Yet, as St. Paul also wrote, "God commendeth his love towards us, in that, while we were yet sinners, Christ died for us" (5:8). Without doubt, that phrase, "whosoever believeth," from the sixteenth verse of the third chapter of John's Gospel, had found its way to me, just as it found its way years later into the hearts of my parents.

Upon hearing that simple good news, I feared for my own soul for the first time in my life. I feared that I might die before someone showed me by means of the Bible how I could be saved. Looking back on it, I realize that salvation was mine the moment I was under conviction, and the prayer I said at the time was its very affirmation. Unfortunately, my aunt, uncle, and cousins lived at some distance from me, in Florence, in the Bitterroot Valley. Because I rarely had opportunity to be with them, I barely grew in Christ. It was not until 1983 that my salvation made sense to me, though to say so during the early stages of my story is to get ahead of myself. For at points between my freshman and senior years of high school I had three more encounters with death.

* * *

One afternoon, while riding my bicycle on South Avenue, I approached an intersection just as a driver pulled out in front of me. Hitting the brakes, I laid my bike down and slid beneath the front of the vehicle. As the car stopped, so did I.

I lay on the road's surface on the front passenger side of the vehicle, staring up at the tire inches from my head and face. In that moment my life literally passed before my eyes. For a split second I thought I was a goner. But, contrary to what common sense might warrant, I did not fear death. Rather, I felt an immediate sense of peace, knowing of my heavenly destiny, had the accident's outcome turned out differently. Yet, the peace was fleeting, for it no longer prevailed once I began to exchange words with the driver!

Yet again, during my senior year, while on my way with friends to a Sadie Hawkins dance, I drove over some railroad tracks not controlled by a crossing arm. Just as my tires bumped over the tracks, my friends and I all but jumped out of our skin as we heard the train's horn blare. We had barely cleared the tracks by mere inches, when from the rear-view mirror we watched it pass. There's a definite reason that some states don't allow several teenagers to be in a car at the same time. Until one becomes an experienced driver, one doesn't appreciate the need for such a law, as I discovered years later as a law enforcement officer. I have heard it said that God looks out for fools, idiots, and drunks. I must admit that during that Sadie Hawkins happy-go-lucky moment, upon the occasion when the girls invite the boys to the dance, I was the fool and the idiot, if not the drunk. Sometimes a man needs a woman to save himself from himself.

During my senior year, I diligently worked at a reconditioning shop for a local car dealership. My primary responsibility was to detail used and new vehicles as they came into the shop. One evening as I worked alongside one of my co-workers, Richard Lamb, I started to fill a compressed air tank with condensed cleaner and water. In my haste to get back to my detailing, I failed to tighten sufficiently the threaded lid to the container. Just then, Richard proceeded to ask me a question. As I turned my head aside to answer him, suddenly the top of the container blew off and hit me squarely in the face. Richard said that the force of the blast had lifted me off of my feet and tossed me backwards some four feet from where I stood. Being momentarily dazed, I reached to touch my face. All I could feel was a warm wet slippery substance I feared to be blood. Fortunately it turned out to be the cleaner from the tank. Due to my careless inattention to the detail of tightening the lid, I received two very black eyes and a broken nose that today still bears the mark of the break. Richard said, "Man, you sure are lucky. If you hadn't turned your head, the top of the canister likely would have driven straight into your nose and shoved the bones right into your brain."

During that same year I decided I wanted to be a police officer, which, given all that had happened to me by then, indicated that perhaps I was the one who needed to receive the policing.

I was fortunate to be offered a one-semester internship with the Missoula Police Department, which was subsequently extended for the entire year. The opportunity to serve my community in a meaningful way greatly appealed to me. I was hooked as I fell in love with the job. The internship required at least forty hours of work each semester, but I logged hundreds of hours before I finished. I had several terrific mentors among the officers, in addition to my primary supervisor, Sergeant Doug Chase, who rose to become chief of the Missoula Police Department and later the sheriff of Missoula County, from which he retired to become chief of the Polson Police Department until finally he hung up his badge and gun.

The dye was cast. As I completed high school, beyond any shadow of doubt I knew I wanted to become a cop. My only question was how to obtain the quickest path to achieve my dream. After speaking with a number of friends in the police department, shortly after my eighteenth birthday I opted for the delayed enlistment program as a military policeman in the United States Army. I was due to ship out soon after graduation. Yet quickly I discovered that things didn't quite go as I had planned.

* * *

After graduation from high school, I made a trip to see my childhood friend Mark, who was working on a ranch for the summer. While passing through the two-dog town of Twin Bridges, Montana, I received a speeding ticket. Later in the month I went to Canyon Ferry Lake where my parents were camping. After considerable persuasion, Dad convinced me to go fishing with him. I hadn't purchased a fishing license because I was about to ship out for duty. As one might guess, as soon as my line dropped into the water, an unmarked boat pulled up beside us. The nice Montana fish and game officer was good enough to share his autograph with me on a ticket issued for fishing without a license.

Still later in the month, when I was about to ship out, I was informed at the MEPS (Military Entrance Processing Station), that a waiver was required in order for me to follow through with my enlistment as a military policeman, simply because I had one too many tickets. The waiver required me to obtain character references from persons who knew me. I soon received several dozen positive responses through the police department. Looking back on it, the ironic thing about the entire ordeal was that even now no record exists for either charge.

I waited from June 1977 until March 1978 for the waiver process to complete. However, my second trip to the MEPS was not without its difficulty. During my physical exam, the doctor informed me that I was too short to be a military policeman, commonly referred to as an MP. A recruit needed to be five-foot-ten, and I was a scrawny five-foot-nine. No less than a mere one-inch difference! And I've always wondered why my recruiter failed to mention that fact. I reminded the physician that I had the right to void my contract, but he advised me to hold my horses. There, again, those cavalry horses! Surely he knew that the modern Army had abandoned those four-legged means of transport.

The doctor asked me to sit tight as he left me dressed in nothing more than my underwear. It was some time before he returned with the station commander in tow. They requested that I follow them into the bowels of a dilapidated basement reminiscent of a 1950s B-rated horror movie. There in the corner stood an ancient scale and a hacksaw complete with recently scattered metal shavings.

I wondered, need I panic? They asked me to stand on the scale and, voila, suddenly I became an inch taller. I signed my contract, took my oath, and off I went to basic training at Fort McClellan, Alabama. At times during the course of the next few months, I regretted my newly found growth to five-foot-ten, not to mention my eagerness in signing the contract.

At the conclusion of basic and advanced training, the Army sent me to Fort Lewis, Washington, the home of the Ninth Infantry Division. There I was assigned, under law enforcement command, to the Ninth Military Police Company. Considering that Fort Lewis was only five hundred miles from my hometown, one would have expected me to be happy. Yet, not so much. At Fort McClellan I had met a person named Penny whom I thought to be the girl of my dreams. She was attending the Women's Army Corps basic training, at the completion of which she received orders to report to Fort Jackson, South Carolina.

It was difficult to get the U.S. Army to change its mind about reassigning someone in order to accommodate a budding romance. Narrow minded, if you had asked me, but nobody asked me. After researching the matter, I discovered that it was possible to take a stateside swap with a fellow soldier if such a person could be found and the respective company commanders were willing to sign off on it.

I eventually located a soldier stationed at Fort Belvoir, Virginia, who was willing to take the swap to Fort Lewis. Because Fort Belvoir was a whole lot closer to Penny than Fort Lewis, I figured I could go see her on my days off. The other soldier wanted to get back to Washington State to be close to his fiancée. My company commander reluctantly signed off on the deal. It took a couple of months before it was approved. Anyone who has been in the service knows how slowly things move when changes to orders are concerned, that is, unless the Army requests them. Our motto was "hurry up and wait."

Ironically, on the eve of our departures we both got dumped by our respective girlfriends. But what we had set in motion could not be reversed, so we each journeyed to our new duty stations. One benefit for me, fortunately, was being deprived of my original deployment to Alaska for the division's 1978 winter training. I missed out on freezing my tootsies and other necessary parts.

My swap mate was not so lucky. He wrecked his truck while going over the Snoqualmie Pass in Washington State, losing his entire Army kit as it cascaded down the mountainside, and without being spared the joy of freezing his nether parts in Alaska.

CHAPTER TWO

Behind Every Good Man Is a Good Woman, Even If He Is Directionally Challenged

"Who can find a virtuous woman? For her price is far above rubies. The heart of her husband doth safely trust in her, so that he shall have no need of spoil. She will do him good and not evil all the days of her life" (Prov 31:10-12).

What for me had been an unhappy outcome with Penny, turned into a blessing in disguise subsequent to my transfer to Fort Belvoir, Virginia. For it resulted in my meeting a wonderful young lady by the name of Carole Coleman who eventually became my wife.

Toward the very end of my advanced infantry training upon the heels of basic training, I suffered an injury during a live-fire maneuver course. Since I was not about to let myself be recycled through all of those dreadful drills again, I gutted out the remaining few days, with most of the cartilage torn in my right knee. Amid my torment I realized something valuable. The many years of observing my mom's struggle with chronic pain had proved beneficial, not so much for her as for me, in that by her courage I learned to persevere through my own pain.

Oddly enough, that military maxim of "hurry up and wait" had proven to be fortuitous. Coincidentally, the day before my knee surgery, in July 1979 at DeWitt Army Hospital, turned out to be the day that Carole and I spotted one another from across the waiting room of the doctor's office. At first glance, I took only vague notice of her as an attractive young woman sitting next to someone I assumed to be her mother. At the time, I was preoccupied with undergoing a second knee procedure, the first having been in January, with unknown consequences for my military career.

I later learned Carole's name, as well as the fact that she was a professional skater, the stepdaughter of her retired stepfather, Tom Forbus. I also discovered that while I was hobbling into the waiting room on my crutches, Carole nudged her mother and said, "He's cute and I'm going to marry him!" as the two then fell into a fit of giggling. Little did they know how far-sighted were those words. Ironically, my parents had met one another in a similar fashion.

The following day, my surgery dragged on longer than expected. Carole, who was next up in the surgical rotation and decidedly nervous, asked the major in charge why it was taking so long. The major explained to her the complications that were causing the delay.

Subsequent to surgery, Carole was assigned to a semi-private room, and I to a ward. It so happened that the men's restroom was situated just past her room, necessitating that I walk by her doorway each time I used the facility. As I did so the next day, she hollered out to me, "Hello, Crip!"

I was not amused. During the past several months following my misfortune, fellow soldiers insistently teased me by calling me "Crip," which I wasn't fond of at all. So, when Carole quipped "Hello, Crip!" several more times, I finally stuck my head into her room and replied, "The name's Chris, not Crip."

We spoke for a few minutes before I walked back to my ward, and then for the next couple of days I paused in her presence with increased frequency as our conversations lingered beyond a mere passing hello. Need I confess that I had no strong objection to visiting a pretty girl all dolled up in her nighty? It's a guy thing.

Carole was released before I was from the hospital, because someone was waiting to care for her at home. I remained hospitalized a few more days before returning to my two-story barracks, equipped with no elevator and with no one to assist me.

Before Carole was discharged, she indicated that she would return to the hospital on Saturday to bring me a gift of cookies. And thus commenced a comedy of errors. The fact that we eventually fell in love at all, and married, was no minor miracle. For, on Saturday when Carole arrived with the cookies, I was out in the courtyard behind the hospital, visiting with another girl I knew. As a stroke of sore luck would have it, there we sat talking as Carole and her mother drove by.

Unbeknown to me, Carole had already been upstairs to my ward. As she and her mother passed by us in her car, I waved. If the look on Carole's face could have killed, then I was flat-out dead, and

I said so to my friend. That night I phoned Carole to apologize. My apology and hunger for sugar notwithstanding, Carole's goodies had traveled back home with her. Only later did this poor, pitiful guy discover that Carole baked fabulous cookies.

* * *

Carole returned to see me the day that I was to be released from the hospital. But before she arrived, I had already been discharged and had set out with an Army buddy for a dinner meal that was a far sight better than any hospital grub. After Saturday's fiasco (best to call it a total flop), I didn't think I'd ever see Carole again. And while I was soon to find out that I was happily mistaken, I nonetheless found myself once more in the dog house, where I've spent plenty of days since.

Believe it or not, an evening or two after my discharge from the hospital, I got a phone call from Carole. She was wanting to know if I'd be willing to come over to her home and offer some help while her mother and stepfather were out for a few hours. I was supposed to arrive there by six o'clock. But, no, it was not to be, for I got lost.

I drove one way all the way south to Front Royal, Virginia, and then all the way back north to Washington, DC—a round trip of 140 miles. Hey, give me a break, I thought. I may be directionally challenged but at least I am determined.

Recall that this was in the dark ages before cell phones. Being a he-man soldier in the U.S. Army, far be it from me to have asked for directions. Clearly, land navigation was not my strong suit. Imagine what would have happened if I'd been at sea.

I finally swallowed my pride and located a pay phone to call Carole. When at last I arrived at her home a little before 9:00 p.m., she met me at the door in her Daisy Duke cutoffs and a T-shirt inscribed, "If you don't like my peaches, don't shake my tree." She was so astonishingly beautiful that I knew this young soldier was in deep, deep trouble.

Things failed to improve for me to any noticeable degree over the next week. Because no one was around to assist me while I hobbled about the barracks, the Army granted me medical leave to fly home to Montana. On the day I was supposed to fly out, Carole was due to meet me at the barracks to take me to the airport. But since I had already checked out early from company quarters, I figured I'd surprise her by going to her home and thus save her the trip. But when I arrived, she had already left.

Fort Belvoir was a thirty-minute drive from Carole's house, so I contacted Carole's mom, Jeanne, at work. Fortunately, for such emergencies I had learned by now to carry spare change for pay phones. While I was speaking with Jeanne, Carole phoned her mom on another line from a phone booth, where she waited for me in a training area of the fort.

I told her mom to ask Carole to stay put and that I would drive there to meet her. I then set forth for the fort and found Carole still waiting for me near the phone booth, visibly upset and in tears because a number of GI's had passed by, shouting cat calls at her. Truth be known she was probably safer than she realized, but I was more than happy to be her knight in shining armor.

We left the base and headed for the airport. But, folly upon folly, when I got to the gate, I discovered that in my haste earlier that day to surprise Carole, I had left my plane tickets in the barracks. If Carole had not already concluded that I was certifiably an idiot, albeit dressed in a service uniform and ready to defend my country should I ever get my act together, then at this point she was thoroughly convinced.

There was no way humanly possible to return to the barracks and get back to the airport in time to make my flight. Nonetheless, we drove to Fort Belvoir to collect my ticket and backtracked to the airport to schedule another flight. By then I seriously wondered whether it would be less insane and more expedient simply to drive to Montana.

Together we returned to Carole's house until it was time to catch the later flight. "Hurry up and wait!" yet once again. Or, in another sense, why wait at all? For by now I was falling head over heels for Carole, although with no assurance that she had even so much as an inkling of falling head over heels for me.

* * *

Thankfully, the rest of the day went well and she dropped me off at the airport later that afternoon. She kissed me goodbye and I headed off to Montana. I figured that any girl who would put up with me so patiently, despite my obvious foibles, must be a keeper. After all that had transpired in such a brief time, her kiss was nothing short of a miracle.

During my trip home I couldn't get Carole off of my mind. After arriving in Missoula, I told Mom that I believed Carole was the one I wanted to spend my life with. I'm certain to this day that Mom was a bit skeptical, considering that Carole and I had known each other for barely two weeks.

During my Montana leave we visited by phone, which happily led me to decide that I would surprise Carole by heading home early to drive her to her best friend's wedding. Yet, I would not do so by showing up unannounced, lest I botch that plan too. When I called to let her know, she was elated.

Sadly, our mutual elation turned into frustration the day I was supposed to arrive in Virginia. I had made it to Great Falls, Montana, all right, but it was at Great Falls that my plane broke down. And there I turned to begging, borrowing, and stealing in an effort to acquire enough change to call Carole on a pay phone. So much for keeping enough change on hand for emergencies! Fortunately, some patrons in the airport took pity on me. They must have figured this crippled GI was down on his luck, and felt sorry for me. When I finally pocketed enough change to call Carole, she wasn't at home. So I called her mother, only to find out that Carole had already left for the airport to pick me up.

When I didn't arrive on my scheduled flight, she returned home in tears, wondering what possibly could have gone wrong this time. Fortunately, her mom bailed me out by explaining the situation. That night, when I finally arrived, Carole met me at the airport with her step brother, Tommy Forbus. She said, "I brought him along in case you didn't show again," and then she added, "at least this time I won't go home alone." And I really couldn't blame her.

From then on, things smoothed out. We attended her friend's wedding; and while the bride was quite beautiful, her maid of honor stole the show despite having to process down the aisle in a walking cast.

By now, Carole had hold of me by the gills—hook, line, and sinker. Admittedly, I was quite happy about being the fish. By September we were engaged, with plans for a May 24th wedding.

While dating, with each of us still on crutches, people would ask us how we both wound up to be crippled at the same time. Our prompt reply was that we had been injured in a three-legged sack race when we took a tumble. Though far from the truth, it made for good theater, staring eyes, and whispered remarks. Before we knew it, the month of May had swiftly become November.

***

While in physical rehab, I was working at the Military Police Vehicle Registration Department. One day—October 16, to be exact—I received a phone call from Carole. She wanted to know how November 17 sounded.

Confused, I answered, "November 17, for what?"

"To get married, Silly!"

Not being the most patient guy in the world, I replied, "Sure. But why the change of date?"

Carole said she had been talking with a workplace friend who had gotten married just before the previous Christmas, saying how much fun the holidays had been.

Looking back on our marriage now, after forty-two years, I can only conclude that Carole didn't want to let a great catch like me get away. Little did she know at the time that she had nothing to fear. I was fully hooked, with line and sinker still in my mouth.

When I asked Carole's birth father, Bob Coleman—Pop, as his kids called him—for his daughter's hand in marriage, after having known Carole but two and a half months, he posed a question that others may have hesitated to ask—"Are you in trouble?"—inferring that Carole might be pregnant.

We assured him we were not. But when we moved up the wedding date, his doubts doubtlessly were magnified. Generally speaking, to marry so quickly, as we did, isn't a great idea. But it worked for us despite the comedy of errors that just as easily could have sent Carole scampering back into the peach orchard as down the aisle to the altar.

Let's just say that when we met, we knew a good thing when we saw one. Our pastor, on the other hand, refused to marry us. So we marched together onto the Army post to get married. We could well have saved ourselves a bucket of heartaches had we listened to our pastor, because it took ten years to make things right with him.

Planning a wedding in the span of one month turned out to be a nightmare. By the end of the month we both had discovered a rather unpleasant side to each other that we hadn't anticipated. Nevertheless, we pulled off the wedding with a lot of help from Jeanne, Carole's mom, and Jeannie Coleman, Pop's wife.

November 17, 1979, turned out to be a beautiful day at the Fairfax Chapel on Fort Belvoir. We pledged our vows before an Army chaplain in the presence of family and friends. We spent the next week on our honeymoon, having a wonderful time exploring Virginia's towns of Williamsburg and Yorktown.

* * *

By April 1980 we were pregnant with our first daughter, Kristi, despite the fact that I was eagerly hoping for a son. Carole's pregnancy was lengthy. Her November due date came and went. When I picked her up from one of her prenatal appointments in December, I found her crying. As she got into the car, she blurted, "I don't think this baby is ever going to come, and if it does come, it will probably be a girl and be born after the end of the year."

Her words were prophetic. Kristi was born in January 1981. We missed our 1980 tax deduction, but I couldn't have been happier than to welcome such a perfectly beautiful little girl whom God had lovingly created for us.

Looking at Kristi now that she had arrived, I tended to forget another side of Carole that I had observed in the delivery room. There she had commented that I would never be allowed to touch her again. I later discovered this to be a common, offhand remark spoken to terrified first-time fathers in delivery rooms. It turned out to be an unfounded concern. For we gave birth to five more children between 1983 and 1988.

Kimberly arrived in 1983. Then Benjamin, born two months prematurely in 1984, went to live in heaven with the Lord. In 1985, Melissa was given birth. Then, Baby Unknown who, under circumstances to be explained, also went to live in heaven with the Lord in 1987. Then, finally, in 1988, Samuel was born.

Carole had wished for six children and I for two. Her desire prevailed, yet with two of our infants abiding in Heaven. And I cannot begin to thank God enough for the four wonderful children he gave us to raise in dedication to him. Unquestionably, they are an abundant blessing to us. The grandkids, in turn, have given us are more than we ever expected or deserved. Our hearts are full.

* * *

While my name is certainly not Abigail van Buren, and no one need address me as "Dear Abby" since I'm not an advice columnist nor especially adroit at dispensing counsel, let me offer some guidance anyway, for the benefit of a few if not all new husbands and fathers.

Here's a tidbit for fathers-to-be, as well as for those who may be bouncing a six-month-old on their knee, as if instructing the tender little rosy-cheek bundle of joy how to stay saddled to a bucking bronco at a country rodeo.

First of all, pay attention to your wife. She is much smarter than we husbands give her credit for being. When you are jostling your infant daughter on your knee and grasping her between your two hands to swing her up from your lap and over your head, beware! Your wife will quickly interrupt you, to say, "Honey, please, I just fed her! Slow down!"

If you are too daft to heed your wife's warning, and laughing with your mouth open, then whatever you do, don't reply with, "Oh, the little darling would never do such a thing to Daddy, would she?" as the formula spews like a volcano all over your face and down your throat.

Just saying!

You see, I always knew that I married up when I married Carole. And I never truly realized just how much this was so until we began walking together with our Lord. As I've grown closer to Jesus Christ, my love for Carole has grown closer too. She is my Proverbs 31 woman. She is an amazingly seamless portrait of Christ's unconditional love for us. She knows me better than anyone, including my strengths and weaknesses; and she loves me in spite of them. She has always stood by me and honored the sacred vows we took all those years ago—a magnificent wife, mother, friend, sister, and now grandmother. It is no wonder that our kids and grandkids adore her as much as I do.

Along this sacred journey I have learned that a Christ-centered marriage is a lasting marriage. Marriage is a one-hundred percent proposition for both partners. Communication is key. Admittedly, in this department I am still a work in progress. It's easy for us to take a spouse for granted if we aren't careful.

We must be willing to face the problems that arise in a marriage and work through them. Every marriage has its peaks and valleys. Seeing the way through the valleys is what makes a marriage stronger. It is far too easy in this day and age to bail out when descending into the first valley. Couples who face the valleys with Christ at their side will grow in love for each other, and grow in their relationship with Christ.

Sadly, too many couples, even Christian couples, jump ship at the first sign of trouble and miss the growth that comes by working through the challenges. I thought for certain that I loved

Carole with all of my heart the day I married her. But I had little idea as to what love truly was to become. My heart has been expanding ever since. I love her more with each new day than I did the prior day when I may have experienced a difficult part of her. It should come as no shocker, then, to know that she loves me when she experiences a difficult part of me.

God commanded, "Husbands love your wives, even as Christ also loved the church, and gave himself for it" (Eph 5:25).

While Ephesians offers no such direct command for wives, it should be clear enough that as men we are to set the tone for our marriages. If we love with a love that is willing to sacrifice of ourselves for the sake of loving our wives, and treat them with the love with which Christ loves his church, then they in turn will love and cherish us.

Military veterans, cops, and firemen understand this. Their camaraderie functions more like a brotherhood and sisterhood, albeit dysfunctional at times. Our very lives depend upon the persons we work with, in the knowledge that we are willing to protect our partners at great cost if need be, including to the point of death. In essence we are a close-knit family. Our marriages should be treated no differently.

I always made a point to take the time to tell Carole and the kids that I loved them before going to work each day. Even if they were out of town, I called them to tell them so. We knew that my job was dangerous. While we hoped that we police officers would not become the victims of danger, we were wise enough to be prepared for that eventuality, including the possibility of never seeing our loved ones again.

During my career, I stared death in the eyes more times than I care to remember. I delivered death notifications to families. I sat with them when their loved ones passed away. Cops are supposed to remain strong and keep their emotions in check, yet I admit that I shed more than a few tears in my patrol car and at home when off-duty. We can't see the terrible things we see and not be affected by them. God gave us emotions for a good reason, and we feel them deeply.

With respect to death, I discovered a marked difference at times between Christian and non-Christian families in their approach to death. While everyone grieves the loss of loved ones, most Christians seem to have a reassuring peace about them, in the faith that beyond death there is an abundant life awaiting them in heaven, as Jesus promised. This is not to say that non-Christians possess no similar hopes for themselves. But it is to say that as a Christian I affirm my faith in Christ by sharing His love with the bereaved. Grieving can be a difficult and prolonged process. But with Christ at our side, grief need not translate into hopelessness.

Looking back, I see how God has worked in my life from my birth to the present. The same is true of my family. Jesus is immeasurably important to us, for it is he who dwells at the center of our life together.

CHAPTER THREE

Not Only the Marines Have Uncle Sam's Misguided Children

At Fort Lewis, which was attached to McChord Air Force Base near Seattle, Washington, I was assigned to the Ninth Military Police Company of the Ninth Infantry Division. Upon arrival, I was shocked to find that my barracks consisted of an open bay similar to the setup of basic training at Fort McClellan, Alabama. A great deal of Fort Lewis's buildings were constructed during or before World War II.

When the time came to depart from Fort Lewis for the swap to Fort Belvoir, Virginia, I was saddened to leave behind my platoon, but I did not miss the dreary clouds that socked in the Seattle area with rainfall for all but a few beautiful days of the year.

As a young military policeman (MP) I split my time between training for war and policing the fort. Duties included standing at the base's entrance gates, monitoring and admitting traffic. I did my fair share of saluting officers' cars regardless of who occupied them. Their teenage children relished the moment, yet we MPs felt a bit silly saluting the military "brats." Other duties included walking a beat at the Madigan Medical Center that contained twenty-one miles of corridors and wards. Erected during World War II, it was designed as a sprawling complex to prevent destruction of the entire facility if bombed by the Japanese. Walking a beat was enjoyable because it involved working with people at ground level. That was how I got my official indoctrination into the unit.

Senior MPs sent the newbies on a mission to the morgue under the guise of locating an official paper or article for an ostensibly important case. Once we newbies were inside the morgue, the senior MP would open two lengthy oblong containers under the pretense of searching for the specified item. Unbeknown to us, the containers were actually vats of formaldehyde containing corpses affectionately known as Freaky Fran and Freaky Freddy, "employed" for teaching purposes at the hospital.

Reactions of the newbies ran the gamut. Some puked, some passed out, some stood still, horrified, and others exhibited no visible reaction at all. One newbie I knew was fearful of dead bodies. He ran out of the room, shrieking in terror. He had definitely chosen the wrong line of work. It took us most of the shift to find the poor soul. While I was surprised but not aghast at the sight of Fran and Freddy since I had encountered death on previous occasions, I passed the test.

Most of the action on my beat took place in the hospital emergency room. There I saw my first gunshot wound. Three soldiers had been off base, traveling in a vehicle. One of them had pulled the trigger of a pistol that lay in the car, not realizing the gun was loaded. The bullet struck the driver in the temple and passed behind his eyes, lodging in the opposite temple. I was stunned not so much by the sight of his blood as by the swelling of his head. The portion containing the bullet looked more like a basketball than a human cranium. I couldn't imagine how painful it must have been. The soldier survived but lost sight in both eyes.

I witnessed a valuable lesson that I had learned early in life during hunters' safety instruction and later in basic training. When someone says to treat all weapons with respect as if loaded, the advice should be taken to heart. During my career I never observed someone accidentally fire a gun, but I did see many people mishandle guns, using them as weapons to kill or maim or discharge them carelessly. A firearm is merely a tool that can be used for evil as well as good purposes.

One night in the hospital emergency room, I assisted a doctor dealing with an unruly and intoxicated non-commissioned officer (NCO) who had been drinking heavily when he got upset with his wife. He had punched out a glass window, which under normal circumstances doesn't typically end well. This was no exception. As the medical officer attempted to stitch up the NCO's hand, he kept jerking it away. No amount of coaxing by his wife or the doctor had any effect. As a result, my partner and I were called to the scene. The medical officer asked us to assist by holding the NCO down.

In a civilian setting the patient has the right to refuse treatment and to leave, but not so in the military where soldiers are the property of the U.S. Army. The term GI stands for

"Government Issue," which means that when an officer orders a subordinate to do something, the subordinate must comply or be disciplined.

As we held down the NCO he continued to struggle. At the very moment that the doctor sought to anesthetize the wound for stitching, the patient jerked his arm and severed an artery in his hand. Blood spurted forth with every heartbeat, spraying all of us. The nurse grabbed a towel and covered the hand, but the blood quickly soaked through it. The doctor then proceeded to knock out the patient with anesthesia in order to finish stitching the wound. What should have been a simple procedure resulted in a court martial offense for the NCO.

Another life lesson was driven home to me that night. Never try to reason with a person intoxicated with alcohol or drugs, for the ability to reason is blunted or blurred. That scenario repeated itself more times than I care to recount throughout my career.

* * *

Should anyone fail to see the pertinence of the Bible regarding the abuse of alcohol, consider the following passage from the book of Proverbs.

> *Who hath woe? who hath sorrow? who hath contentions? who hath babbling? who hath wounds without cause? who hath redness of eyes? They that tarry long at the wine; they that go to seek mixed wine. Look not thou upon the wine when it is red, when it giveth his colour in the cup, when it moveth itself aright. At the last it is bitter like a serpent, and stingeth like an adder. Thine eyes shall behold strange women, and thine heart shall utter perverse things. Yea, thou shalt be as he that lieth down in the midst of the sea, or as he that lieth upon the top of a mast. They have stricken me, shalt thou say, and I was not sick; they have beaten me, and I felt it not: when shall I awake? I will seek it yet again."*
> (Prov 23:29-35)

Whenever on domestic calls, I observed first-hand the destruction to families caused by the abuse of drugs and alcohol. On the street I found drunks in some of the oddest places. I witnessed havoc, pain, and death inflicted upon families whose members were killed by drunk drivers, including the families of those drunk drivers.

I lost a friend, Officer Steve LePaine, to a drunk driver. His death motivated me to become what some of us refer to as a DUI hound.

During my career I personally arrested about 300 people and processed nearly four times that number when working on DUI teams. It wasn't for pleasure. DUI processing is a meticulous and often unpleasant procedure. It's time-consuming and takes an officer off patrol for long periods. I truly believed that every drunk taken off the road was potentially one life or multiple lives saved. Early on, the majority of those I arrested were first-time offenders. Sadly, by the end of my career most were multiple-time offenders. In spite of the good work of police officers all around this country, as well as wide-spread public media campaigns, deaths from drunk driving are just as prevalent today as when I first became a cop.

One particular late-night shift was extremely slow. I struggled to stay awake. I was driving back to the MP station on the base in heavy early morning traffic, when momentarily I dozed at the wheel. A mild jolt abruptly awakened me as I looked up to realize that I had just bumped into the car in front of me. The other driver hopped out and met me between the two cars. Neither vehicle was damaged. He apologized for stopping so quickly. I decided to roll with it and said, "That's okay, buddy, just don't let it happen again!" With that I got into my patrol car and drove off.

I sweated that encounter for a couple of days, thinking I had lucked out, until one of my sergeants happened to stop by my bunk and ask me about it. It turned out that he was a friend of the guy I had bumped. Because no damage was done to the vehicles, he let me off the hook with a stern warning, and then together we laughed.

As a rookie, I decided from there on out, no matter how minor the issue, it was important for me to file a report with the shift sergeant. Honesty is always the best policy to live by. I was reminded of the saying from the book of Numbers, "Be sure your sin will find you out" (32:23b). There is no escaping the eyes of the Lord. He does not expect perfection, but he does expect us to live godly lives as much as possible. The Holy Spirit dwelling in our hearts convicts us of sin. Confession and God's forgiveness free us and transform us.

* * *

My senior partner, who shall remain nameless, and I, were out together on patrol when we received a call regarding a loose barking dog. It was not the first time the dog had been a problem. As before, the owners were not at home. After the fiasco of trying to capture the "offender," we eventually placed it in the back of the patrol car. Animal control was off shift, so we made our way to the shelter on post. As we drove, the canine refused to exercise his right to remain silent, to my partner's utter frustration.

Suddenly the "subject" made his way to the front seat, which was not in its best interest. A deadly silence prevailed as the four-legged escape artist made its way out the driver's-side open window. My partner then radioed dispatch about the dog's rapid escape, a serious offense.

Being the newbie on board, I yielded to my senior officer's judgment and his request that the case be closed. I cannot divulge whether or not the "fugitive" received a helping hand out the window, or, whether anyone conducted a thorough search for the "escapee." Let's just say that while I was stationed at the post, we never received another complaint at that address. Maybe the "escapee" had returned home or was captured and taken into custody after I transferred elsewhere at the end of my service. Who knows?

I trust People for the Ethical Treatment of Animals did not lose any sleep over the incident.

***

By then, the situation at Fort Lewis had turned decidedly downhill for me. My right knee, which I had busted up in basic training, had really begun to bother me. It became necessary to report my injury, which resulted in my being assigned to light duty, with the admonition that I take care of the knee as soon as I arrived at Fort Belvoir for my pending swap.

I undertook the long drive across the country with a stopover in Missoula to visit my family. We celebrated an early Thanksgiving and Christmas together, and I headed out again on the road. I made a brief stop in Harlowton, Montana, to visit my Uncle Harold and Aunt Eva Edwards, my mom's sister, as well as my Grandmother Abney, my mom's mother, who had recently been diagnosed with inoperable cancer. The visit was sweet but heartbreaking, for I knew this was likely to be the last time I would see her alive, which it was.

Uncle Harold and Aunt Eva took me out to dinner the night before I was to depart. They treated me like royalty, being quite proud of my service to our country. Sadly, when we said our goodbyes, I didn't know it would be the last time that I would see Uncle Harold too. He died of a heart attack not long after my departure. I learned of his and Grandma Abney's deaths soon after arriving at Fort Belvoir. Because I had used up my available leave for the stateside swap, I was unable to attend their funerals.

While on my trip east from Montana along Interstate 90, a troublesome trend developed that has haunted me ever since. I discovered that I was directionally challenged, in case it was not already obvious. Unfortunately, the invention of GPS did not cure the mysterious curse, but at least made it easier for me to get back on track after going astray.

I was supposed to catch Interstate 80 out of Chicago. But being the Montana country bumpkin that I am, I plumb missed the turn. I was one hundred miles or more out of Chicago on my way to New York before I realized my mistake. Need I say that my trip to Virginia was a wee bit longer and more exasperating than it should have been? The delay was largely the result of my inattention. After all, I had just recently lost my girlfriend. Or, at least, that was my excuse and my story. And I'm sticking to it.

The rest of the trip proceeded without mishap. However, to this day my branch of the family tree is known as Turnaround Schultz's. I regret to say that I have passed along my defective directional gene to some of my children. While honesty is the best policy, it's also downright embarrassing.

* * *

At Fort Belvoir I was assigned to the 521st Military Police Company under Training Command. Though considerably smaller than Fort Lewis, Fort Belvoir also had two MP companies, the other being the 437th which split MPs' time between field duties and post duties. In the 521st we were tasked with full-time law enforcement on the post, referred to as "white hat duty" because of the white saucer caps we wore with our class A uniforms. In my mind, we looked more like bus drivers than cops. Our duties involved patrolling the fort, guarding the access gates, and staffing the post's vehicle registration office.

From November to January, I worked the post patrol and the gates, while a military surgeon evaluated my knee. During that time I discovered the joys of the South's winter humidity since Fort Belvoir was located in Alexandria, Virginia, on the Potomac River forty minutes from the eastern coastline. Montana, on the other hand, which customarily experienced far less humidity, was miles upon miles from the Great Lakes and the Atlantic and Pacific Oceans.

    The 437th MP Company issued cold weather gear to its members since they conducted field exercises. Unfortunately, the 521st did not, since we worked exclusively on the post. Being in a patrol car on a wintry day was one thing, but working the gates in the crisp winter air was quite another. A few of my fellow soldiers suffered minor frost bite. I survived the ordeal mainly because I was accustomed to the dry cold of Montana winters, although my posterior, hands, and feet all too often felt numb. We were told that the heater inside the guard shacks would be sufficient to keep us warm, but the post command apparently forgot the requirement that we stand outside the gate, greeting incoming and outgoing traffic. During daylight and early evening hours, the traffic was nearly non-stop. I soon learned that freezing temperatures were nature's way of testing my military mettle, and I was none too impressed.

* * *

The post's golf course was located adjacent to the main gate. I came to appreciate some of the more dedicated players' determined and relentless pursuit of the game. More than once, I stood at the gate and watched those poor souls hit and chase tiny fluorescent orange balls in the snow while I shivered in my jump boots. I wondered why anyone in a sound mind would be so eager for voluntary punishment of the flesh in deep mid-winter. Then it occurred to me that quite possibly the same sadistic post officers, who refused to issue us cold weather gear, were just taunting us. I like to play golf as much as the next guy, but I prefer planting my feet on sturdy turf warmed in the summer sun at the local mini golf park. Taking a golf swing while slipping on icy footing is not exactly the way to heal an injured knee.

    In January 1979, the surgeon performed open surgery on my right knee for the first time, to remove most of the cartilage. I spent the next several months in physical therapy, which would have been better described as physical "torture" inflicted by ghoulish, sadistic practitioners of a dreaded medieval profession. In spite of their efforts, I saw little improvement. I did learn to isolate and exercise my knee muscles quite well, if anyone happened to be interested in seeing a good flex-show while I was wearing my shorts.

    The doctor wouldn't yet release me for full-time duty, so I was assigned to the vehicle registration office on the post. You might, although I couldn't, imagine my excitement. But I had my dad to thank for teaching me that any job worth doing is worth doing right. So I rolled up my sleeves and got to work. I determined that I would not be a sour-faced, monotone paper shuffler standing listlessly behind the counter, as at most vehicle registration offices. The assignment actually proved to be useful. It helped me learn to talk to people from all walks of life even though I longed to be back on patrol.

At last, in July, my surgeon decided to cut into my knee for a second time. I had continued to experience episodes of knee-locking and swelling from fluid that needed to be drained, a method of torture all its own level. Let's just say that it's an awesomely unforgettable experience to have a strawberry milkshake drawn from your knee with an excessively large needle and equally large syringe. After the second surgery, when the remaining cartilage was scraped out, I walked bone-on-bone. Surprisingly, within a few months I was back on patrol.

* * *

While patrolling, I discovered that there were two sides to the Uniform Code of Military Justice. One applied to the officer corps and the other to the enlisted ranks. Two separate DUI arrests, the first and second of my career, demonstrated the difference.

The first instance involved an Army first lieutenant whom I stopped after observing him weaving all over the road. He miserably failed the basic sobriety tests. His breath had the distinct odor of an alcoholic beverage, and he admitted that he had been drinking. Per protocol, I contacted my shift lieutenant who soon arrived at the scene. As part of my briefing, I advised him of the danger that the suspect represented to others on the road.

My shift supervisor opted for returning him to his billet and ordered me to drive the offender's car for him. However, I was not allowed, nor did my supervisor choose, to arrest him. Because I felt that it was wrong not to have done so, whether or not the offender later received the Army's punishment, I questioned my supervisor as he drove me back to my patrol car. He said that he had not wanted to ruin the officer's career, so I had no choice but to accept his verdict.

After a month or so went by, I stopped another young soldier under similar circumstances. I put him through the standard sobriety maneuvers and conducted an interview. The only difference in his case from the earlier one was that he had a small bag of marijuana in his possession. The shift supervisor responded, and I arrested the soldier who then got hammered by his company commander with Article Fifteen military punishment, as well as by the federal judge to whose court I cited him. There was no regard given to how his arrest and punishment might affect the young soldier's career. At the end of the day, I was still glad that I had done my job by taking two drunks off the road. But I was appalled by the double standard, for the Uniform Code by no means had been applied uniformly. The inebriated officer in the first instance posed as much of a threat to the motoring public as did the inebriated enlisted soldier in the second instance.

Victims of accidents suffering injury to themselves or the death of loved ones and friends are not concerned with the rankings and career promotions of irresponsible drivers who are to blame for their irresponsible behaviors. Police officers should not be concerned either. Like Lady Justice wearing a blindfold and holding the scales of justice in each hand, police officers should enforce the law fairly and evenhandedly without partiality or favoritism. I suspect that Lady Justice was thoroughly disappointed by the unequal justice dispensed in those two cases.

* * *

Happily, guard duty at the gates was not always about misdeeds and misdemeanors. The act of saluting one another was so deeply ingrained that at times we developed a warped sense of humor about it. We took great care to salute officers promptly and with heightened decorum whenever they passed through the gates, or whenever a passing vehicle displayed an officer decal. I saw officers knock cigars and cigarettes out of their mouths while attempting to return a salute. On more than one occasion I feared a wreck might ensue as an officer grabbed a lit cigarette lest it set fire to the officer and the car. Such scenes were ready-made for TV commercials pitching anti-smoking campaigns, and would have made for jaw-breaking laughter on Americas Funniest Home Videos.

My all-time favorite incident occurred one bright sunny Saturday morning. Without having the slightest idea as to his actual name or rank, for he was wearing civilian attire, I decided to name him Colonel N. Picker. He had his index finger shoved up his nose so far that I wondered if he was aiming to scratch a brain itch. With his finger still firmly planted in his nose, he raised his hand to salute. I burst into laughter. I couldn't help but imagine the unseemly outcome—a wrecked car, a ripped nose, and a cracked skull.

What explanation would he give to the brain surgeon?

***

While I was stationed at Fort Belvoir, the 437th Company and members of the 521st were called to assist with the reception, protection, and screening of the Cuban boat people who migrated to the States when Fidel Castro emptied his prisons and insane asylums of his political prisoners.

This caused a logjam for our Immigration Department and the need for the Army to set up temporary quarters at Fort Indian Town Gap, Pennsylvania, to house many of the asylum seekers. Those of us who stayed behind at Fort Belvoir endured twelve-hour shifts for the next several months. We operated with a skeleton crew and with very few days off. While this was not easy, it prepared me for the many long hours I would often have to work when I eventually became a civilian police officer.

With Carole being pregnant with Kristi at the time, and my being about fourteen months shy of the date of my separation from the Army, I received orders to be transferred to Korea. This meant I would miss Carole's due date. While I was not averse to going to Korea, I didn't want to miss my daughter's birth. So I exhausted every avenue to get out of the orders, but in the end resigned myself to the overseas tour, unaccompanied. Every service-member knows of this possibility when signing up to serve, and from that standpoint I had no reason to complain.

About a month before I was scheduled to leave, a friend visited me from Levy section, the office responsible for processing troop orders and assignments. It was located next to the vehicle registration section where I had been assigned while convalescing after my second knee surgery. My friend requested that I come to her office on a specific day. So I met her on the front steps where she handed me a paper containing the deletion of my orders to go to Korea and the continuance of my assignment at Fort Belvoir.

She said not to ask any questions, so I turned and walked away, thankful for her help. As in the Vietnam-era TV series *Mash* about the Korean War, my friend proved that Radar O'Riley was still very much alive. For Radar always managed to present the solution to a problem before anyone asked for it. Like Radar, I wondered, how did my friend know of my orders to Korea, and how did she pull off their deletion? I left well enough alone, deciding not to look a gift horse in the mouth.

Then, with only eight months of my enlistment remaining, I received orders to Korea yet again. This meant I would have to extend my enlistment by four months. But with different plans in mind for myself, I chose not to increase my time in the Army. The colonel in charge of the battalion then tried to talk me into staying and extending. He said that I would have a difficult time finding an appointment outside of the service. I opted, however, not to follow his advice. In April 1981, I left active duty, saying what turned out to be a temporary goodbye to my military career.

In 1982, I enlisted in the Virginia National Guard to serve for the coming year in the 116th Infantry out of Manassas, Virginia, before returning in 1983 to Montana. There I transferred to the Montana National Guard's G Troop of the 163rd Armored Cavalry, as a crewman on an M60 A2 tank.

I also worked simultaneously for the Missoula City Police Department. Unfortunately, my police shifts didn't coincide with my Guard drills, and I was unwilling to burn up all of my vacation days playing army, no matter how much I liked it. Although I drilled at the armory on my days off from the police department, I was repeatedly passed over for a promotion for not having trained with the unit.

I have often wished that I had stayed in the Guard for its additional retirement benefits, but family life was more important to me.

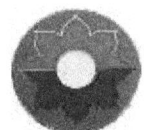         

9th Infantry Division 9th M.P. Company Ft. Lewis, WA. 1978.	TRADOC Command 521ST M.P. Company Ft. Belvoir, VA.	116th Infantry VA National Guard Manassas, VA 1982-1983	163rd Armor MT National Guard Missoula, MT 1978 1983-1986

* * *

Backtracking to 1981, I worked that year as a part-time night-shift security officer for an outfit named Wells Van Meter Security. I patrolled active job sights, unfinished subdivisions, offices, shopping complexes, and apartments owned by the company. During daylight hours I worked security for the Mount Vernon Hospital of Alexandria, Virginia.

Everyone has heard the expression "look before leaping." This was never so true as the time when my night-shift responsibility with Wells Van Meter included keeping an eye on the model homes in a sub-division under construction, surrounded as they were by four-foot fencing at the entrances. Because the gates were locked and we had not been provided with keys, access meant vaulting over the fence in order to check all the doors and windows to ensure they were secured.

Deep darkness had set in after a downpour of rain. Being unable to see what lay on the other side of the fence, I vaulted over and landed on the ground to a loud squishing sound beneath my right foot, causing me nearly to slip and fall. Glancing down with horror, I noticed a very large bull frog that had exploded instantly from the force of my 170-pound body. I had planted my right heel squarely in the middle of poor old Kermit's back. My boots and pants legs were covered with his remains.

After finding a hose to rinse off, I nevertheless stank of frog guts for the rest of the night, not to mention the pronounced squishing in my boots as I walked for the rest of my shift. It was quite apparent that any hopes I had of sneaking up on any would-be thieves or burglars that night would have been impossible. With my sincere apologies to People for the Ethical Treatment of Animals, I certainly did not intend to commit frog-slaughter.

* * *

Working at Mount Vernon Hospital in its security department also had its bizarre moments. Often we were called to the psychiatric ward to assist with unruly patients, in addition to making daily rounds and checking on the staff.

The Fairfax County Police had brought in a particular patient the night before, and it had taken several officers and staff to get the patient into a padded room for his own protection. Once he had settled down, my shift had the task of letting him out the following morning. He was, as we often said, a "frequent flyer" to the ward and invariably violent when he arrived. Once he was back on his "meds," he normally turned docile. But on this occasion we stepped up our patrols for the next few days just in case.

I referred to the patient by the name of Hopeful. For each time we went onto the unit, we noticed Hopeful walking tirelessly in circles around the nurses' station at the center of the ward. This continued for several days until the thought finally occurred to me as to why he walked in circles around the nurses' desk. In my pea-picking mind I determined that it was because he was attempting to wear out the floor in an effort to make the nurses' station collapse into the floor below it, which would then allow him to escape. I figured it was probably as good a theory as any.

One afternoon, Hopeful managed to slip out through an unsecured door with a female patient whom I'll call Ready. When security was notified of the breach, we commenced a search of the hospital for the two would-be love birds. Within several minutes we located them in a janitor's closet in separate stages of undress. Let's just say that we made sure the outcome did not result in an untimely pregnancy. While they were definitely two peas in a pod, we spared them of receiving the parents-of-the-year award—Hopeful and Ready—or not.

Another "frequent flyer" we dealt with on a regular basis was a deeply disturbed individual who had experienced a recent breakup with his girlfriend. She had called the Fairfax County Police to request a welfare investigation of him because he had threatened to do bodily harm to himself. When the police arrived, they found that the man had severed his male appendage and was bleeding profusely. The officers accompanied the ambulance to the hospital where the emergency room physician inquired as to the whereabouts of the appendage. Since the officers had not thought to secure the item, they returned to the residence only to discover that the victim's dog had helped himself to a delicious meal, which by the time its remnants were returned to the hospital were mangled too much to be reattached. The ex-girlfriend who made the call to the police felt so sorry for the fellow that she ultimately married him. Given his psychological issues, I have my doubts that it remained a long and fruitful union.

Dealing with inpatients in the psychiatric ward always made me feel uncomfortable. While I realize that mental illness is definitely a reality, so is demon possession, which I observed from time to time throughout my career. As a Christian, incidents of demon possession, while not common, do occur. The incident just described was such case, and it caused the hair to stand up on my neck.

Satan will use just about anything at hand to destroy a life. I was reminded of words from the First Epistle of Peter: "Be sober, be vigilant; because your adversary the devil, as a roaring lion, walketh about, seeking whom he may devour." (I Pet 5:8).

I admit that I can only speculate as to what drove the man to do what he did to himself, yet I can't help but think that a battle raged deep within his soul. Saint Paul wrote: "God says, What?

Know ye not that your body is the temple?" (I Cor 6:19). When Satan destroys the body, he is much closer to destroying the soul.

I had no idea as to how widespread mental health problems were in this country until I worked at the hospital and later with the court system. For police officers, emotionally disturbed persons (EDPs) can be challenging to work with, and sometimes impossible. Law enforcement does not take lightly EDP calls, due to the potential for violence. Many an officer has been injured or killed by an EDP. Sadly, many an EDP has been injured or killed by a law enforcement officer. It is an area that requires yet more education and training of police officers, medical personnel, and mental health workers. At the same time, cops need to see the humor in things that frequently are not so humorous, in order to offset the ugliness to which cops are exposed.

Another task of security officers is to move bodies to the morgue when someone has passed away. While I was working an evening shift, the victim of a shooting involving the police had to be removed from the emergency room. The deceased had been implicated in a double homicide in another county when it was reported that he was located at an address in Fairfax County. He had made statements saying that he would not be taken alive. He held true to his word. After being given the chance to come out peaceably, he decided to come out shooting. I was at the morgue when detectives took photos of the body. One officer had shot the suspect with a 38 Special while another officer had shot him with double-O buck from a shotgun. The suspect didn't go down easily. He took six rounds at center mass of his chest from the 38, and the double-O buckshot wasn't far off center. I was impressed with the accuracy that both officers had exhibited. In many a Hollywood film the bad guy goes down with one shot. But real life often presents a much different scenario.

These were the sorts of jobs I undertook while processing my application with the Prince William County Police Department in Manassas, Virginia.

I had attempted to return to Montana, but no one was hiring at the time. Carole mentioned that I may as well work locally until something opened for me back home. At that particular time, the Prince William County Police Department was hiring one person for every 300 applicants. Despite the odds, I applied and was chosen to be one of four officers fortunate enough to join the force.

Once again, God continued to look out for me.

CHAPTER FOUR

High-Test Patterson, the Listerine Man, and Moon Mullins

In the fall of 1981, I started working with the Prince William County Police Department. While waiting for my training academy to begin the following January, I went through an orientation, after which I received my uniforms and equipment and was assigned Officer Bill VanCuyk as my field trainer.

Because of my previous military police training, I proceeded straight to the street with Bill. Without hesitation, he quickly became one of my greatest mentors. He had been a New York City police officer assigned to Brooklyn for fifteen years prior to taking early retirement due to departmental downsizing. He left the city in order to get away from its crime. His home had been burglarized twice in his last year on the job. During the second burglary, he watched the perpetrator exit the front door and descend the stairs, carrying some of Bill's uniforms. This was no environment in which to raise his six daughters.

Bill was a no-nonsense, friendly training officer who expected me to learn. He taught me to write thorough reports and good tickets, and make solid arrests. He said that if I did those three things well, I would not spend a lot of time in court; and when I did have to go to court I would likely win. I lived by that advice for my entire career and it never failed me. Bill taught me how to remain safe so that I had the best chance of returning home each night. He really took me under his wing. I couldn't have asked for a better training officer as my first. We became partners and friends over the next several months, which were among the best of my career.

I wrote and rewrote more reports under his tutelage than I care to remember. He taught me the art of verbal articulation and how to construct a logical sequence. The hardest task during my first days of training was learning to understand his thick Brooklyn accent. While I never could speak "New Yorkian," I did come to understand him. If Saint Paul's relationship to Timothy were to apply to law enforcement, then Bill VanCuyk was my Saint Paul.

Embarrassing things happen to all rookies and I was no exception. Little did I know then that I would soon become an expert of sorts with respect to the art of rookiehood. Initially, I was issued used uniforms until my new ones arrived, some of which were threadbare. I did not realize just how threadbare until I was about to step out of our patrol car one afternoon while on a call.

Most of us know the frightful sound of fabric ripping. In my case the rip was from my belt loop to the bottom of my zipper, which exposed my rear-end to a fresh gust of wind. Consequently, I had to ask Bill to take the lead. This alone was excruciating enough, apart from enduring Bill's sudden burst of laughter at my expense. But he took it all in stride.

After we completed the call, we drove to a fabric store where he purchased a needle and thread—that, too, at my expense. You can imagine my embarrassment as I sat in the cruiser in my underwear, sewing up the butt of my uniform trousers, all the while fearing that at any moment we would receive a call to respond to an emergency. I became a quick study. From then on, I kept a needle and thread packed in my gear bag. If a uniform gives a rookie a newly found sense of self-importance, then a rip of the pants definitely lessens it. Then, too, if God was paying as much attention to the state of my trousers as to the state my ego, then he knew the perfect way to keep me humble.

* * *

During our times together on dispatched calls, Bill and I met some very interesting people. One of the first was a guy by the nickname of High-Test Patterson. For non-NASCAR fans, high test is a grade of gasoline.

High-Test Patterson had a peculiar habit of turning up in some unusual places in various stages of undress, accompanied by a can of gasoline. Customarily, he was as high as a kite from sniffing the fumes. For the most part, he would go with us peacefully, but he also had a propensity to be a bit ornery. I had encountered him frequently over the course of time. While he was the ripe old age of a man in his mid-twenties when I first met him, of late I could have sworn that he didn't look a day over fifty. But unless High-Test seriously changed his ways, he would soon be sniffing his way to the big petroleum factory in the sky.

Another upstanding citizen I had met was known to officers as the Listerine Man. His modus operandi was to buy that age-old breath freshener, Listerine, whenever he could afford it or otherwise shoplift it. He always maintained that it was "the good stuff." One day Bill asked him, "Why Listerine?" He replied, "I used to drink Aqua-Velva until they ruined it by putting the green stuff in it." I soon came to believe that marijuana was a gateway drug. Perhaps, too, Listerine and gasoline are gateway drugs to Tequila and jet fuel. The lengths to which people go to fill an emptiness in their brains and hearts is incredible. Yet, when you stop to think about it, gateway drugs are no match to a personal relationship with Jesus Christ for filling that emptiness.

* * *

One of my first public-disturbance calls with Bill was about a fight that had broken out at a place called the Silent Clown, a notoriously anti-cop establishment with a history of some grand disturbances. As was true then, whenever we received the distinctively southern "Y'all come" call to respond, every car in the area headed the same way. Arriving on the scene, I observed an amazing display of unbrotherly love involving an altercation between two brothers whose names I remember to this day but will not divulge just in the unlikely case they miraculously became honest citizens.

The older of the two had taken hold of his brother upside down by the ankles. As we drove up, we noticed he was repeatedly bouncing his brother's head off of the asphalt with a *ker-thunk* each time it hit the ground. We grabbed the older brother to pull him off. Then the younger brother's instinct to protect his big brother kicked in. Before the episode was over, both of them wound up in handcuffs in the back seats of cruisers where they proceeded trying to kick out the windows.

In those days it was acceptable to hog-tie arrested persons to prevent them from injuring themselves or others. The procedure involved placing a set of leg irons around the ankles and drawing the legs up to the hands. Just so, due to their persistent threats, we and another car transported the miscreants to the magistrate's office into which we carried them in hog-tied. The magistrate found it difficult to speak to them in their hamstrung position on the floor, so we sought to lift them to the counter where they could be more easily addressed. When this proved unhelpful because of their anti-social demeanor, the magistrate signed the warrants and off they went for an all-expenses-paid night in the gray bar hotel.

The following evening when we arrived for our shift, we learned that the two scrappers had accused us of police brutality. I, for one, saw my short career pass before my eyes. I knew we hadn't done anything wrong, yet it was unnerving to have a complaint filed against us. We had merely restrained the pair. None of our officers had so much as thrown a single punch.

Bill assured me that we had nothing to worry about. He believed we would eventually be exonerated. Our squad sergeant was put in charge of the investigation. Then a miraculous thing happened when the sergeant went back to the Silent Clown to get the skinny on what had occurred the night before. As I said, the establishment was not known for its love of law enforcement. Unfortunately for the brothers, however, a multitude of witnesses came to our defense, including the bouncers who before our arrival had already thrown the brothers out of the bar for their abhorrent behavior.

The following day, our sergeant spoke with the brothers at the station and advised them that they were within their rights to sign a complaint, but that a number of witnesses had come forth to exonerate the officers. Should they wish to continue with their complaint, the sergeant advised them that he would be more than happy to arrest both of them for making a false police report. The brothers considered their options and made their first intelligent decision within the prior twenty-four hours, choosing to drop the complaint. I suspect that they may have feared winding up back at the magistrate's office, once again hog-tied on top of the counter.

* * *

One night, Bill and I received an "officer needs assistance" call to a house party. A K-9 officer in our unit had chased a subject into the party, only to be surrounded by an unruly crowd trying to free the person. The entire shift responded to the K-9 officer's call for help, setting up another embarrassing rookie moment for me.

Bill was first out of the car when we arrived at the scene as I struggled to untangle myself from my seatbelt. As soon as I cleared the seatbelt and the door, I leapt from the car, thinking to myself, here I come to save the day! I had taken but two or three steps when I heard from behind me an awful clanking of metal. I looked around just in time to see my Smith and Wesson Model 64 .357 magnum revolver bouncing on the concrete. I stopped to retrieve it and then followed Bill to the house party.

Once the call was over, I examined my gun only to discover that it was scuffed on each side. At the time, the department was issuing the border patrol's old snap-over holsters. The snap apparently had got caught on the seatbelt and the gun's grip, releasing the gun from my holster as I ran. On the bright side, I received a brand new weapon to replace the damaged one. The next day I purchased a level-two retention holster. A weapon bouncing once during a career was more than enough.

* * *

One evening I was already off shift and preparing to go home when the dispatcher advised that there was a domestic disturbance occurring in an apartment complex. Additional information indicated that the male subject possessed a semi-automatic rifle and was threatening to shoot his spouse and any cops who showed up at the residence. The late-night shift was running short-handed, so Bill and I and a few other officers volunteered to go as back-up. The suspect's wife advised us that her husband had seen us arrive and had fled from the apartment with his rifle. To the side of the complex stood a patch of woods and numerous other buildings. So we cautiously began our hunt for the suspect.

As I searched the area just below the tree line, I heard Bill yell the command, "Put down your weapon!" Shortly, Bill and another officer emerged from the woods near me with the suspect in handcuffs. Bill said to me, "It must be your lucky day." When I asked why, he explained that the suspect, who had been concealed inside the tree line, was taking aim at me through the scope of his rifle just when Bill spotted him.

A chill ran down my spine as the suspect announced, "I would have had you if I hadn't forgot to load my rifle." We later discovered his fully loaded 223-caliber, 30-round magazine at the house. I thanked God that the guy was intoxicated at the time. But for the man's clouded thinking from the alcohol in his system, this memoir would have remained unwritten and my budding career reduced to a line or two in my obituary.

* * *

I experienced many firsts with Bill, including my initial encounter with an incidence of suicide when we received a call to check out a suspicious vehicle a few days before Thanksgiving. When we arrived at the scene, we could see someone slumped at the steering wheel. At first, thinking the person asleep or drunk, I cautiously approached the driver's side and peered inside, only to spot a revolver in the victim's hand. Startled as I was, not by the weapon but by the gore of his self-inflicted head wound, it proved that a holiday for some pour souls can turn out to be anything but happy.

At the time, I didn't understand what might drive someone to take his own life. But years later, I came to appreciate the fact that stress can be a terrible and irresistible demon, even for someone who has developed a personal relationship with Christ as his savior, but who strays from the abundance of life that Christ has to offer.

On another occasion, the dispatcher directed us to where the nude body of a young white woman lay at the side of a county road. Wrapped around her neck was a piece of her own clothing. Her paleness and lividity indicated she had been dead for a while. Lividity occurs after death, when the blood pools in the body at its lowest points. In this case it had pooled in her legs, back, arms, and buttocks where those body parts touched the ground. To the untrained eye, lividity appears like bruising.

As was the case then, I am invariably struck by the inhumanity of people who murder fellow human beings. How can anyone so callously kill another person and dump her alongside a deserted road like a heap of discarded garbage? With my mind's eye, I can still see her lying there as if it were today. Would that it had been the last time I saw such horror.

* * *

Bill was also a crime scene technician. After completing the phase of field training that followed my time at the police academy, Bill assisted me with the first fatal accident I encountered, which involved a pedestrian walking along a state road when he was struck by a van.

That day, the driver of the van had just finished a job that required several extra hours of work. He had momentarily fallen asleep at the wheel and drifted towards the side of the road where the intoxicated pedestrian stepped over the shoulder line and into the traffic. Upon hearing the thud from the impact, the driver awoke to see the pedestrian sprawled out on his hood. By the time he was able to stop the van, he had dragged the victim's body some distance.

When I arrived at the scene, there was not enough left of the man's corpse to be able to identify him. Yet I was drawn to the tattoo on his arm. Its placement suggested that it belonged to a character I had arrested on a warrant a few days before. I couldn't help but think that, had he not been released on bail, he would still have been alive.

As we investigated the crash, Bill and I noticed a strange white line on the surface of the road, leading to where the body lay. Upon closer inspection we determined it was the skid mark from the victim's skull that had been dragged beneath the under carriage of the van.

Later that morning I was to leave on vacation. The image of those mangled remains and the skid mark were not what I wanted on my mind as I set out to drive my family across the country. The wreck reminded me of the fragility of life. For in the blink of an eye, two unrelated lives suddenly had become tragically linked. And the driver of the van was destined to live with that day's catastrophe for the rest of his life.

***

Every police officer deals in his own way with the horrors of the job. As for myself, I tended to compartmentalize them in my mind. It may sound rather callous, but my way of coping was to look at the deceased not as a person but as dead meat. By doing so, I detached from the horror of the moment long enough to do the work at hand. Later, after returning to the comfort of my home, I allowed myself to wonder about the person, and what the person must have experienced before dying. I didn't necessarily dwell on the matter for long, but as a Christian I reflected upon the person's eternal whereabouts. Earlier in my career I had vividly recalled each corpse I had seen, but those morbid preoccupations for the most part had slipped away, that is, until I retrieved some of them while looking back at my own story.

My work, however, has not always been about death and sadness. Invariably, lighter moments have produced chuckles that now and again resurface for their lasting and sometimes humorous impressions.

One such "impression" was of a bubble in a windshield that a human head had struck upon impact. I had just rolled up on the accident. Below the head-shaped bubble appeared a tiny but prominent bubble that puzzled me. Only after speaking with the front-seat passenger did the wee bubble make sense to me. For I noticed that her forehead not only sported a significant bump and scrape, but, in addition, a broken nose. The image of her nose became clear as I pictured it buried in the windshield. I have seen hundreds of similar accidents, but I have never come across another one that I would describe as having involved Ms. Pinocchio.

At the scene of another accident, I observed a phenomenon that I had heard of before, but never witnessed. Some poor soul had been walking in the middle of the road when he was struck by a fast-moving vehicle that instantly killed him. The guy had been wearing a pair of laced-up work boots that, after he had been propelled several yards away, were left standing right at the spot of impact, as if he had just stepped out of them. While apparently not an uncommon occurrence, it definitely gave a whole new meaning to the expression "boots on the ground."

* * *

Through Bill VanCuyk I learned that, with few exceptions, most criminals are not Rhodes Scholars. Case in point.

Bill and I were dispatched to a burglary one morning while on day shift. While investigating the crime scene, we discovered a wallet at the point of entry. A shard of glass impaled in the window contained fibers that appeared to be from blue jean material.

I affectionately referred to the intruder as Lucky Lou, who had made off with a number of items that made it appear as though he had committed the crime of the century. We eventually found a phone number for Lucky, and I called him.

I inquired as to whether he had lost his wallet, to which he readily replied that he had. "Well," I said, "I have good news for you. We have it here at the station, and all you need to do is come down and pick it up." He seemed glad that it had been located.

He arrived at the station as happy as a clam, ready to retrieve his wallet. Bill and I then escorted him to an interview room where we read him his Miranda rights and asked him about the burglary. Lucky assured us he knew nothing about any burglary and had never heard of the business. We pointed out the tear in the pocket of his jeans and told him where the wallet had been found. For a finishing touch, we asked him what the odds were that the fabric we had recovered at the scene might match his jeans that we were about to seize. Then the sky opened up and the angels sang. Lucky suddenly remembered having been at the scene and committing the crime, and confessed his transgression. As a bonus he even helped us get the stolen property back. A stand-up guy after all!

* * *

When I was working for Prince William County, my territory was split into two districts, with the one district centered in Manassas and the other in the Garfield substation at Woodbridge. During our shifts we were often called to meet the Garfield Substation officers at the Independent Hills State Police Barracks, which was the halfway point for prisoner transfers to the jail.

Most of the time the transports were uneventful. However, one sticks firmly in my mind. The prisoner was an eighty-plus year old who had been arrested on the charge of public drunkenness. The fellow was a happy-go-lucky Irishman quite short in stature. Aside from the black suit and derby he wore, he reminded me of a leprechaun. He greeted me with the statement, "'Tis a fine evening, officer." I greeted him in-kind and we set off to the jail.

About two minutes into a twenty-some minute drive, my leprechaun piped up from the back seat and said that he had "ta shite." At first, I wasn't sure what he meant. So I quizzed him a bit, to which he responded, "Ya know, Laddie, I need ta shite—use the crapper, Lad."

Once I understood his meaning, I panicked. There was no place to stop before reaching the jail. I then asked him if he knew any Irish songs. "Aye, Lad," he said, "I'd be happy t'sing some fer ya!" Over the next few minutes he settled into singing songs that I did not recognize, but which as a lover of Celtic music I enjoyed. I felt quite proud of myself for being so smart as to distract the leprechaun from his present dilemma.

However, my pride was short lived. The old fellow became instantly quiet. Then I noticed a distinctly unpleasant odor emanating from the back seat, followed by, "I'm so sorry, officer, but I shite me pants. I couldn't hold it in," which was an understatement. I opened the windows, stuck my head out, and got to the jail as quickly as possible. When I dropped him off, he was still apologizing. I guess it's true that when you've got to go, you've got to go—true even fer leprechauns.

Upon leaving the jail I rushed to the nearest fire station. The firefighters were gracious to offer me a hose, some disinfectant, and a doughnut, which I declined under the circumstances while hosing down my seat.

For some inexplicable reason, the prisoners who rode in my back seat in the next two days complained that it smelled like a hospital, and wondering if possibly they had wet their pants just before getting out of the car.

* * *

During my time at the academy, we watched videos on what not to do as police officers. In one clip of a Hollywood-produced training film, officers transported a rather boisterous prisoner in the back seat of a patrol car. When the prisoner refused to quiet down, the officer asked the guy if he wanted to be a star. After a moment of silence, the man asked, "What?" when suddenly the officer behind the wheel abruptly slammed the brakes on the car. The poor guy immediately flew forward into the separator screen. The training maneuver was known as a "screen test." The film served its purpose, for I made a mental note to always buckle in my prisoners before transporting them.

And this brings me to the night I was on patrol, when I noticed someone in the middle of the road, staggering, falling, rolling, and then somehow managing to get back up on his feet, only to repeat the exercise. When speaking to him, I recognized him as one of our regular "frequent flyer" alcoholics. In addition to being highly inebriated and smelling like a pot factory, he was also deaf and mute. Since I didn't know sign language, communicating with him was out of the question.

For the sake of telling the story, I shall name him Joe. Since he lived several miles away, there was simply no way I was going to leave him in the middle of the road to become an ornament on the front of some unsuspecting driver's hood. So I did the only logical thing. I arrested him for being drunk in public, handcuffed him, and placed him in the back seat of my patrol car. Then off we went to jail.

But something nagged at me—something I could not put my finger on until we came to the railroad tracks as we entered Manassas. I was clipping right along at a fast pace because of a call I had received, to which I needed to respond. As my cruiser bumped over the tracks, I suddenly realized that I had forgotten to buckle in Joe with a seatbelt. To my horror, through the rear-view mirror I saw poor Joe flying forward, planting his face, nose, and cheek squarely into the screen, and then sliding down it like Wylie Coyote in a Road Runner cartoon. When we arrived at the jail a few moments later, Joe was still trying to come around from his daze. So much for what I had learned from the training film, with little chance that Joe would make it big on the Hollywood big screen!

* * *

The rookie year is supposed to be the first year. But in all fairness to rookies, I'd say that it encompasses the first two to four years. Good cops know that they never stop learning and are never quite as good as they think they are. Striving to improve and to learn from mistakes is a career-long endeavor.

One of my most memorable mistakes occurred as I was making a DUI arrest of a driver with a car full of teenagers. From the very outset, the fight was on. Being in a remote area, my nearest backup was at least fifteen minutes away. The suspect kept screaming at his friends to help him. I could tell by the expression on their faces that they were seriously considering his request. Having secured one cuff on the driver, thinking I had control of him, I then made my mistake. In haste I reached for my shoulder mike to request assistance.

As the radio transmission partly died out, I lost my grip on the suspect. The next thing I knew, I was on my back against the trunk of my cruiser, with the suspect freely swinging the other cuff at my face, trying to disfigure my handsome good looks.

Seeking to regain control as I warded off his blows, suddenly there appeared the form of someone who looked like the Incredible Hulk, absent the green hue. He lurched toward us from the darkness. Seeing his bearded face, I hoped he was a cop. And, sure enough, it was Dickie Jenkins, one of our narcotics officers, who instantly grabbed the suspect by the scruff of the neck and forced him into the cruiser's trunk. Rookie lesson learned! Finish handcuffing before calling for backup!

On yet another night, I came close to being hit head-on by a drunk driver. After turning around and stopping the guy, whom I've nicknamed Baby Huey, I noticed him unfolding himself from the front seat of his compact car. I still don't know how he managed to get in and out of the thing. Fortunately, he was a gentle giant. I later felt almost sorry for arresting him. Most people who are stopped for drinking and driving have been to some cigar-box law school that instructed them to say, "I've had only two beers." Baby Huey was no exception. After quipping to him, "Those must have been pretty large beers, considering your size," he endeared himself to me by replying, "Yep, it was two full pitchers." One just can't help but appreciate honesty.

After another nearly head-on collision, I stopped the driver of a vehicle for driving under the influence. A husband-and-wife couple were coming from a Christmas party in Washington, DC, with the wife driving because her husband was intoxicated. It was a thoughtful courtesy on her part, but she was as much or more intoxicated than he. They both said they worked locally for a federal agency that shall remain nameless. I made the mistake of saying, "Sure, and the next thing you are going to tell me is that you are rocket scientists."

It's been said that a good attorney never asks a question to which he doesn't know the answer. A smart-aleck rookie should do the same. In fact, they truly were rocket scientists and had the credentials to prove it. Both of them went to jail that night, she for the DUI and he for public drunkenness. Due to his pride, he failed to provide me with the phone number of a sober person to come and get them. They may have been rocket scientists, but some things don't require rocket science. They require common sense.

* * *

One Friday afternoon, I sat in front of the Manassas National Guard Armory, shooting the breeze with an Army buddy, when a frantic citizen drove up to tell me about a drunk driver in a semi-tractor and trailer, which I had just happened to see drive by. The complainant stated that the truck was running people off the road, and the driver was hurling beer cans out the window.

I admit to being a bit skeptical. Nevertheless, I went after the truck to investigate. As I caught up with it, I was surprised to see that it was forcing several vehicles off the road. Very soon, out popped a beer can through the driver's window. Indeed, the complainant had pegged the guy accurately.

At my direction the semi finally pulled over. As I approached it, walking along the driver's side, I noticed the driver watching me through the side mirror with a crazed look in his eyes. Upon reaching his door, with the hair standing up on the back of my neck, I ordered him out. He instantly looked at me as if he were contemplating his next move. After I issued repeated orders for him to get out of the vehicle, he complied. I then put him through the field sobriety tests that indicated he was definitely intoxicated.

When I sought to place him under arrest, the fight was on. We skirmished all the way to the rear of the truck until I finally handcuffed him just as my backup arrived. The suspect possessed no license. The truck was apparently leased to a different name than the one he gave. Refusing to reveal his real name, he maintained that he was Moon Mullins (a comic-strip moonshiner from the 1920s.) The trucking company eventually confirmed his true identity.

Before transporting Moon from the scene, I walked back to the cab of the truck to get his registration and insurance information. It was then that I noticed a loaded Ruger 357 magnum revolver sitting on the truck's console. I immediately understood why I had been concerned about that contemplative look on his face. Undoubtedly, he was considering whether or not to shoot me.

I am thankful for the angel sitting on his shoulder, which discouraged the devil sitting on his other shoulder. From then on, I learned to trust my body's warning signs. If something doesn't feel quite right, then it probably isn't. (As a footnote, a Ruger 357 magnum revolver turned out years later to be my nemesis.)

I suspect that Moon Mullins went down in the annals of Prince William County as one of the most expensive DUI prosecutions on record. Moon was charged with a plethora of transgressions. In addition to the DUI, he was charged with resisting arrest, assault on a police officer (for which he also had prior arrests), driving with a suspended or revoked license, and reckless driving. Moon failed to appear for his first court hearing and was later arrested on warrants for all of those charges.

Once arrested, Moon insisted upon his case being heard in circuit court. After several continuances, it was moved from the general district court to the circuit court. His attorney apparently got wind of the fact that I was leaving the police department to return to Montana, so he figured he would ride out the matter until I was gone. Then he might get Moon's case dismissed. Little did the attorney know that Moon's antics and his own would raise the ire of Virginia's commonwealth attorney.

Two or three months after arriving in Montana, I got a call from that commonwealth attorney, saying that I had been issued a subpoena to return for Moon's trial, with all of my expenses paid by the state. Yet when the day for Moon's trial arrived, Moon did not appear.

Moon's girlfriend and two of his friends were present in the courtroom. When the trial began, Moon's defense attorney asked that both attorneys be allowed to approach the bench. As I watched a muffled discussion ensue between the judge and the prosecuting commonwealth attorney, the judge's face turned red with anger. Moon's attorney then walked away from the bench as the judge advised the court that the defense attorney, at his own insistence, had been removed from the case. As he passed by me, Moon's attorney reached for my hand to shake it, and whispered, "Sock it to him!"

I hadn't heard that expression since the sixties, but I figured it must be a good sign. To say the least, the commonwealth attorney and I were dumbfounded. The judge stated that due to the numerous continuances, the trial of Moon would commence in absentia. After the commonwealth attorney's opening statement, the judge asked for witnesses for the defense. Moon's girlfriend and his two friends raised their hands.

One by one the judge called them to the stand. All three stated that Moon had approached them, asking them to lie on his behalf by saying that they had been with Moon all day, and that Moon had not been drinking. Moon had also asked them to state that I, Chris Schultz, had stopped Moon for no reason except to beat him up. As each one testified, the judge's anger welled up all the more. I subsequently presented my own testimony in support of the commonwealth's case against Moon.

At the conclusion, the judge found Moon guilty of all charges and sentenced him to more than two years in jail, with each sentence running consecutively. He fined Moon the highest amount he could for each charge and then tacked on court costs, including the expense of bringing me back for the trial. It was a sad day for Moon when he was eventually arrested.

Among the Ten Commandments, God declared, "Thou shalt not bear false witness against thy neighbor" (Exod 20:16). I cannot claim that this biblical injunction against bearing false witness was the motive behind the witnesses' refusal to lie for Moon. But whatever their reasoning, I am glad they chose to speak the truth.

* * *

You never know what a night on patrol will bring. That is half the fun of the job and why, above all other assignments, I preferred to be on patrol except when I was walking the beat. Each call, each contact, each traffic stop, was different.

One evening I was checking out an area off the beaten path, known for drinking and drug activity. After dark, I noticed a suspicious car occupied by a driver and passenger in a closed lot. I asked them to step out of the car. I checked them for weapons and began to prepare their field interview cards. I had completed the information for the first person and asked the second for his driver's license. When he handed it to me, he stated, "Okay, officer, but you aren't going to believe it."

My heart skipped a beat when I saw the name Theodore Bundy on the license—not the infamous criminal, Ted Bundy, but a poor unfortunate soul whose parents thought they had given him a good and honest name. Little did they know that their son's name would turn out to be synonymous with that of the diabolical serial killer.

Not only did my heart skip a beat, but so did the dispatcher's and everyone else's on the air, as well as the folks at the National Crime Information Center. Within minutes I had several backup cars alongside me and an FBI agent on the phone with the dispatcher, wanting to know Bundy's and my location. A driver's license check, plus a call to the prison where the notorious criminal was housed, verified that Bundy was safely tucked in for the night in his cell. As I said, you never know what a night on patrol will bring. Nor can you make up this stuff.

* * *

On a beautiful sunny Sunday afternoon I was dispatched to a property dispute between neighbors. The homes in question were off the beaten path out in the sticks. The complainant said that he and his neighbor had been at odds over a fence that the complainant had built close to the adjoining property line. He advised me that his neighbor was unusually confrontational that day and thought he had been drinking. As we stood talking at the fence, the contentious neighbor, a seventy-some year-old male obviously intoxicated, approached us, cursing up a blue streak. So I asked the complainant to wait inside while I discussed things with this irate neighbor.

I stood patiently as the old fellow, who seemed perfectly harmless despite his spate of foul words, vented about the fence and what he perceived to be an uncooperative next-door neighbor.

It was then that I made an almost fatal mistake, for I did not ask the old man to keep his hands out of his pockets. He then said to me that if that (expletive) son of a so ever set foot on his property, he would kill him—at which point he pulled out of his pocket a 25-automatic pistol and pointed it directly at my face only inches from eyes.

My first thought was to drop, draw, and shoot. But I sensed that he might perceive my movement as a threat and might pull the trigger before I could move out of his line of fire. So I looked calmly at him and said, "Hey, partner, I don't think you really want to point that thing at a police officer," wherewith the old man gasped, dropped the weapon to his side and apologized profusely.

Alcohol can cause an otherwise intelligent person to do stupid things. In police vernacular we refer to this phenomenon as "add alcohol, and poof, an instant idiot!"

Having a gun shoved in your face can cause you to fill your britches, not that I did so to mine. But on the positive side, it caused me to realize that anyone, even a harmless-looking senior citizen, can be dangerous if you let your guard down. I learned never to take anyone for granted. As cops we have a saying: "God looks out for drunks and idiots." In this instance who was the idiot for letting his guard down? The *lucky* idiot?

* * *

Perhaps the worst chewing out I ever received was near the end of my second year with the department. I had responded to a call about a fight taking place in one of our local drinking establishments. Its business name stated that it was a Family Restaurant, yet it was anything but. For it was known as a hangout for outlaws and wannabe-outlaw biker gangs.

We had a standing operating procedure that no one was to enter such a place without a backup unit standing by. While on my way there, I failed to pay attention to the direction from which my back up was coming. Yet, because I had seen emergency lights a block away, when I arrived I opted to go into the business to stop the fight. About halfway inside I encountered the two culprits and broke up their fight by grabbing each of them by the back of the collar. By then I was wondering where my backup officer was.

The crowd was getting ugly, so I pushed both suspects to the back door which was the closest, only to find it locked. I then turned around and headed back through the crowd, with both suspects still chipping their teeth at one another, which is to say, arguing. Fortunately, they wanted to fight one another and not me.

As I passed by the bar, someone from the crowd reached to grab my weapon from my holster. With my large Maglite in my right hand and my left hand grasping the suspect by the collar, I instinctively slammed the Maglite down and instantly heard a howl of pain. I did not have time to see whose hand I had hit, so I shoved both suspects out the front door with several patrons following me.

To my shock, the emergency lights that I had mistakenly thought to be my partners were actually those of the fire department.

So there, squarely before me stood four firemen taking bets on whether or not I would come out of the place alive, wondering who this fool cop was. I could only plead temporary insanity, because no one other than an insane person would be stupid enough to let happen what had just happened.

Later, when my corporal arrived, I received a well-deserved chewing out, which to this day makes it hard for me to sit down. For I swear that all of one butt cheek and a good portion of the other are still missing.

Standard operating procedures are meant to protect us, not hinder us. Some of us learn the hard way. Some of us never learn. Others die from stupid mistakes. It was my lucky night, however, and I've never forgotten it. As for the person who grabbed my gun, he was quickly long gone. My perverse hope is that still to this day he possesses a well-warped hand, courtesy of my flashlight.

I am truly amazed that I lived through my rookie years. I was fortunate to have angels watching over me. I really can't offer any other explanation for my unwarranted good luck. Sadly, many young officers and even some senior officers have made the ultimate sacrifice as the result of a rookie's mistake. Life and longevity are not guaranteed. Law enforcement is a dangerous and now-and-then an unforgiving profession.

* * *

There are many more hair-raising stories that I could tell, but to bring this chapter to a close I'll mention a few lighter notes.

While on the day shift one afternoon, I was working traffic in one of my favorite fishing holes. I observed a vehicle speeding, so I set up a pace on it. Having followed him and verified his speed, I pulled up behind him and turned on my lights. Let's call this guy Speedy.

Speedy did not accelerate away from me, but neither did he stop. After following him for another two miles, he pulled into the driveway of a residence, and I pulled in behind him. As I got out of my patrol car, Speedy announced that he was home safe. This was a new one for me, so I said, "This isn't baseball," and proceeded to ask him for his driver's license, proof of insurance, and vehicle registration. He complied and I wrote him a ticket from the trunk of my car. After I explained the citation to him, Speedy went into his house.

I was feeling pretty cocky about the stop until I proceeded to get back into my car. I was aghast to realize that I had locked my keys inside along with my radio. Every cop knows that, had I had my radio, I would have been reluctant to use it for fear of being harassed by my shift mates.

I was located on a country road with the nearest house in either direction being about a mile. After considering my options, I came to the embarrassing conclusion that I was going to have to swallow my pride and knock on Speedy's door to ask for a clothes hanger. I paused at the door for few moments before knocking. When speedy answered I explained my dilemma and asked to borrow a coat hanger. Needless to say, he laughed at me and asked if I was going to tear up the ticket. I said that as much as I wanted to, I could not do so because I had to account for every citation. Speedy let me squirm for a few minutes before handing me the hanger and then continued to laugh the entire time I was breaking into my car. The last laugh was Speedy's at my expense.

After leaving his house, I went directly to the hardware store to have a duplicate key cut. I vowed never again to be trapped in a similar situation. To this day I carry an extra key with me as insurance against the possibility that, just when I think what a sharp cop I am, God may humble me for being not only keyless but clueless.

* * *

Periodically, we had to attend in-service training at the police academy in Fairfax, Virginia. At the time, I was stationed at the Garfield substation in Woodbridge, which is in the East end of Prince William County. At the conclusion of each day's training I would drive from the academy in Fairfax back to my work at the substation.

As I drove along I-95, headed for Prince William, I noticed a driver I shall name Mr. Dipstick. He taunted me by pulling up beside me and then dropping behind me, only to repeat the maneuver again and again.

Once we drew close to the Prince William County line, Mr. Dipstick floored the accelerator and jumped to eighty miles per hour. I thought that if Mr. Dipstick wants to play this game, then who am I to let him down? So I pursued him over the bridge that enters Prince William County, and for another mile and a half before he abruptly pulled over to the side of the road.

When I approached his vehicle, Mr. Dipstick demanded to know what I thought I was doing by stopping him. He stated that he was now in Prince William County and that therefore I had no jurisdiction.

Because he seemed somewhat confused, I pointed him to my badge and asked him to read it. I then showed him my shoulder patch and asked him to read that as well. And I was seriously tempted to walk him to my car and ask him to read the emblem on its side. But I decided that might be overkill.

Mr. Dipstick steamed as I wrote out his citation. When he left, he was still steaming and saying how unfair it was of me.

Actually, his confusion was understandable. For Prince William County's patrol cars were typically aqua blue and white in color. Fairfax County's patrol cars, on the other hand, were more of a navy blue and white. That particular model year Prince William County decided to purchase some darker blue cars with white roofs, which lent some confusion as to which county they belonged to.

The illustrious Mr. Dipstick thought that he had me right where he wanted me. I suppose you could say that he had burned the oil in his engine down to the level where the friction from pushing the petal to the metal finally caught up with him. For having disregarded the rules of the road, Mr. Dipstick's pride hath steameth before the fall.

* * *

Police officers are known for pulling practical jokes on fellow officers. Of course, a true professional, like me, would never consider stooping to such crassness. Scouts honor, toes crossed!

I was working an accident one morning on a rural road. One of my zone partners was assisting since the accident occurred on a blind curve. It was just before dawn when, all of a sudden, I had to go to the bathroom.

My dilemma was such that the tow truck was at least fifteen minutes away. And, on top of it, I was at least ten minutes from the nearest restroom. And we hadn't seen a single car for at least that long.

Being the conscientious officer that I was, I always kept a spare roll of toilet paper in my bag. So up the hill I went with the roll in hand.

Now, mind you, it had been raining, and I had my handy-dandy, department-issued, bright yellow glow-in-the-dark rain slicker on as I hiked thirty yards up the hill and stepped behind a small tree, facing the road. Relief was in sight.

As I dropped by pants and squatted over a fallen log, suddenly the sun came out over the ridge top, illuminating me for all the world to see. Not that it mattered much, because my illustrious, faithful partner had shined the patrol car's spotlight onto the tree and me *just as a string of fifteen cars rolled around the corner to find me crouching in all my glory.*

Of course, it was a practical joke. But somehow it served to remind me that, no matter where we are, and no matter what we do, we cannot escape the all-seeing eyes of God. The words of Jesus are worth considering if we think we have anything to hide.

> *There is nothing covered, that shall not be revealed; and hid, that shall not be known. What I tell you in darkness, that speak ye in light: and what ye hear in the ear, that preach ye upon the housetops. And fear not them which kill the body, but are not able to kill the soul: but rather fear him which is able to destroy both soul and body in hell. Are not two sparrows sold for a farthing? and one of them shall not fall to the ground without your Father. But the very hairs of your head are numbered. Fear ye not therefore, ye are of more value than many sparrows. Whosoever therefore shall confess me before men, him will I confess also before my Father which is in heaven. But whosoever shall deny me before men, him will I also deny before my Father which is in heaven."* (Matt 10:26b–33)

* * *

Given the number of miles we drive on patrol, it is no surprise that police officers have occasional accidents, and yes, some of them are their own fault.

One rainy night I received a BOLO (be on the lookout) call over the radio for a possible drunk driver on State Route 234 in Manassas. A vehicle matching the description had just driven at a high speed by the cross street where I had stopped at a 711 for a Big Gulp and a bag of microwave popcorn.

I turned behind the vehicle and then accelerated to catch up in order to look for any sign of the driver's impairment. Heading downgrade along the four-lane highway, unbeknown to me a pool of standing water lay at the bottom of the hill.

At the last moment the subject shifted lanes.

Being busy watching him, I missed what should have been obvious yet crucial information. So, when I hit the water, the patrol car hydroplaned and spun out of control.

Having noticed that the oncoming lanes were clear, I figured that at least I wouldn't hit another vehicle. Yet I failed to see the light pole in the middle of the dished-out median. And the next thing I knew, I had wrapped my right-front fender around it.

Imagine, if you will, the Big Gulp situated between my legs, and the open bag of popcorn resting on the passenger seat. An interesting phenomenon occurs when an object in motion (the car) abruptly stops. Any unsecured items within it continue dashing forward at the speed of the car. Thus the popcorn scattered all about and my soft drink distributed itself throughout, dripping from the headliner, pooling on the seat, and splashing into the crotch of my pants.

When my sergeant arrived, he was not at all sympathetic toward my plight. He took one look at the inside and then the outside of the car, resting as it was in the median with its flashing light bar only slightly higher than the road surface, and he uttered, "Go to the office and we will talk there!"

He may have been a little more forgiving had the patrol car not been in need of a full detail job in addition to repair of the damage from the accident. This minor impropriety cost me two days off.

On the bright side, I was sent back through the pursuit-driving course which I was allowed to take during those two days off, without pay. The course was nearly enough fun to make up for the reduction in my paycheck. In most calamities there is a silver lining in the absence of a gold one.

* * *

What I am about to say could come under the subtitle of "A Son-in-Law's Revenge." Mind you, I have a great relationship with my father-in-law. As for you cops who may not have such a great relationship, I suggest that you ask your dear old dad-in-law to spend an entire shift with you on a busy day.

That was the case one afternoon when my pop-in-law, Bob Coleman, sought to venture out with me to see how well I supported his daughter and grandkids. It was an especially eventful day requiring several code-three runs, or, shall we say, moving at one hundred fifty miles per hour.

Don't panic, I was actually driving slower than that. But one hundred fifty miles per hour will get your attention.

Since Pop wasn't the biggest guy in the world, his hind end levitated off of the seat as we navigated a couple of hills. His defiance of gravity seemed rather cool to me since I'd never known Pop to be a magician.

At one point he looked a bit green as he hung out the window. If I wasn't mistaken, he was engaged in a moment of prayer. I wondered what could have precipitated his sudden urge for spiritual guidance. Yet, all the same, I appreciated his prayer for me as well.

With Pop being a NASCAR fan, I figured that he probably had an irresistible urge for speed. While it is one thing to watch speedsters from the comfort of an easy chair or the grand stand of a speed park, it is quite another to do so from the front seat of a squad car.

Let's just say that speeding through traffic left Pop white-knuckled, gripping the dash and edge of his seat. Premature graying runs in the family. In his case the rate of change ran its course during one day's patrol shift.

Most of all, we had a wonderful time between calls, discussing the issues of life and solving the problems of the world through thoughtful discourse. That is, it was wonderful until the second half of the shift when Pop grew extremely quiet.

I had been under the impression all along that Pop had had a good time while riding with me that day. But then I wondered why he never expressed the desire to ride with me again.

Surely, it wasn't because of those code-three runs—my revenge—was it?

* * *

Bidding adieu to Prince William County at the conclusion of my second year with the department, I took a vacation back to the Big Sky country of Montana. While there, my mother suffered a massive heart attack. It was her second in two years. The first had occurred while I was at the academy. I had younger brothers still at home. The bulk of my family lived in the area.

I began looking for a job that would take me back there permanently. I discovered a two-man police department in the town of Stevensville, Montana, that was looking for an officer. The department had gone through seventeen officers in the past few years. This should have set off a warning light for me, but my heart wanted what my heart wanted.

I saw the job announcement on a Thursday in the local Missoula paper. So I picked up an application the same day and turned it in on Friday. I interviewed the chief on Monday and was hired the coming Thursday night after my meeting with the town council.

I left Missoula on Friday to return to Virginia, where I gave my two weeks' notice and then set off into a new chapter of our family's life.

CHAPTER FIVE

Mayberry Is Not in Montana!

I had never really considered the culture shock that Carole was about to experience. We moved across the country from the congested northern Virginia metropolitan area to a small rural town in Montana with a population that upon the moment of our arrival grew from 1,200 to 1,204 people.

Stevensville was not totally devoid of modern technology, for it had its very own traffic light. For fun on a sultry summer night, we could sit at the intersection and watch the light as it changed back and forth from red to green, until the person behind us ventured to disturb our solace with a honk of the horn.

During the first two weeks, I trained for the job and learned to navigate the city under the tutelage of Police Chief Lou Barnett. Lou was a good guy and an exceptionally good detective, which I figured had something to do with his gift of gab. He was well known among his peers and just about everyone else in the Bitterroot Valley.

I made a year's commitment to Stevensville, with the intention of applying to the Missoula Police Department should applications open there. In the meantime, I familiarized myself with Montana law and my new work environment. That first year was both interesting and challenging as I negotiated the politics of that small community.

In order to obtain my Montana POST (Peace Officers Standards of Training) certificate,
I had to attend two weeks of training at the Montana Law Enforcement Academy in Bozeman, where I learned Montana's State codes for criminal and traffic law. I also had to qualify for the use of my handgun and shotgun. Once completed, Montana accepted my previous training and POST certificate from Virginia.

As part of the state's requirement to maintain certification proficiency, two Missoula County deputies attended the same in-service training along with me. One of them was Sergeant Allen Kimery, with whom I developed a friendship based upon mutual Christian beliefs. Little did I know that only a year later Allen would make the ultimate sacrifice for his community by giving his life in the course of duty.

In a small town everybody knows everybody, and most of the time everybody's personal business as well, including what you do and where you live. I had been in Stevensville only a short time, when one evening while I was off duty a panicked neighbor knocked at my door to say that in the bowling alley a block behind my house a man was not breathing.

I had no time to suit up. So I quickly drove to the bowling alley and on the way called the 911 emergency service. Upon my arrival, I saw that another neighbor, an EMT and volunteer fireman, was administering CPR to the man. When I asked him what I could do, he asked me to take over the mouth-to-mouth resuscitative breathing.

In those days we didn't know about AIDS, so masking was not part of the protocol. As everyone's eyes watched to see how this new officer would perform CPR, I knew that my reputation, and likely my livelihood, was on the line.

As I was about to bend over to begin the process, I saw where the man had already vomited. To top it off, his beard consisted of at least two days' worth of stubble. And then, when I offered the first several breaths, he vomited again. So I swept his mouth to clear it. Breathing for someone who was puking was not high on my bucket list of things to do before exiting the stage, but it had to be done. I choked back my own nausea while being as professional as I could, praying that I'd not puke in front of everyone.

We brought the victim back to life for a few seconds and then he fell into full arrest and died in spite of our efforts. I learned later that he had suffered an aneurism that had blown out the back of his heart. Our efforts basically pumped him dry, which we had no way of knowing at the time. That evening I discovered that he was a former Stevensville police chief.

Throughout my rest of career I performed CPR four more times, each time without wearing a mask. My success rate remained at zero, despite being told by medical personnel that I had done everything as I should. By my observation, two of the victims I assisted were already deceased, yet I rendered CPR for the sake of loved ones who were clinging desperately to hope. While the CPR hardly helped in that situation, it seemed like the right thing to do.

Parenthetically, if anyone were to need CPR from me now, let's just say that it would be best not to hold out high expectation for the chance of survival.

* * *

A month or two into the job, I was dispatched to a residence for a reported domestic disturbance. When I arrived, I came with all lights on my vehicle blacked out so as not to alert the suspects to my presence I walked in from the end of the long driveway leading up to the house.

About halfway, I came under fire. The first round snapped by my head like a buzzing bee. I stood on open ground with no cover, and not at all sure from where the gunmen was firing. So I ran a zigzag pattern back to my patrol car from which I called dispatch about the shooting and waited for backup.

There is nothing quite like a bullet zinging past your head to motivate you to seek cover. I don't know how fast I made it to my car, but I'm sure the speed was my personal best.

The shooter was a juvenile who had taken his girlfriend and her family hostage over a break-up that he believed to have been precipitated by the girl's parents. (I have heard it said, and I believe it to be so, that most if not all teens, especially the males, are basically brain dead from the time they turn thirteen until they reach their early twenties.)

The incident evolved into a several-hour standoff, with the suspect wandering in and out of the house with his weapon. He never again pointed it at any of us, but the situation remained tense until he finally agreed to surrender. I suspect that the young lad's actions didn't improve his prospects for dating the girl again anytime in the future. If he had only stopped to think about his foolish action beforehand. Holding the entire family hostage was not the smart way to win their hearts and affection.

* * *

The chief of police and I both had our own patrol cars. They were hand-me-downs purchased from the state, well-worn when we received them. The cars' badges were the magnetic, slap-on type, and of course thoroughly high tech. Because of some local miscreants, we never knew at the beginning of a shift just where on the car we would find those badges. Yet, on the bright side of things, while the badges were frequently displaced, they never disappeared.

One night about midway through the year, due to a highly flammable situation, the police chief lost his patrol car. At the time, I was riding along with a friend from the Missoula Police Department, when I received a call to contact the chief.

The chief explained that he was in hot pursuit of a vehicle when his antiquated and overly used patrol car caught fire. He was lucky enough to remove a few personal belongings and his shotgun before the car became fully engulfed in flames. He also managed to save the car's high-tech magnetic badges. It was not until several months later that he received a replacement car. In the meantime we hot-seated mine, which meant we shared it. Thus, the car never got a break and its hot-seat never cooled.

Stevensville was far from being a hotbed of crime, but with its close proximity to the cities of Missoula and Hamilton it was rarely deprived of its fair share of wrongdoing. The unique thing about working with a small department was that we were assigned to every possible job, including patrol officer, detective, crime scene tech, and public service officer, all wrapped into one. As a result, I broadened my horizon, worked each case from start to finish, and felt a definite sense of accomplishment when the case was closed. While bigger cities may have possessed more high-tech bells and whistles than we ever laid our eyes on, I found throughout my career that it was often within the smaller jurisdictions that patrol officers gained a more well-rounded experience. Larger departments were compartmentalized, preventing their patrol officers from broadening their knowledge of new aspects of the job.

The two of us officers in the Stevensville department were always on call. My wife and I had our daily routines down to a science. I could awake from a deep sleep and be in uniform and out the front door within four or five minutes. Carole would be standing there, handing me my gun belt and kissing me goodbye with her tender loving words, "Be Careful."

* * *

One night, I received a burglary-in-progress complaint from our local pharmacy. In just under six minutes I was on the scene. I planned to block the main entry with my car and run by foot to the only logical exit. As I pulled up, I realized that the complainant had given the dispatcher the wrong point of entry, for the perpetrators had come in through the backdoor instead of the front. Since I lacked immediate backup, I wished to give the appearance that two officers were on the scene instead of one.

As I rounded the side of the building, the suspects had already taken off down the alley. Knowing that they had the advantage since I was without assistance, I waited for support before searching the alley. But by the time the support arrived, the suspects were long gone. So much then for making a timely arrest.

I eventually learned that an informant had divulged the name of the primary suspect to the chief of police, and that both suspects were armed. At least one of them had no compunction about killing a police officer. But once he knew that law enforcement was on to him, he fled the state.

* * *

Another night I received a call to remove someone from a resident's house. The subject turned out to be a local alcoholic who deserves the distinction of being called Freddy the Freeloader.

A Good Samaritan and his Good Samaritan wife had felt sorry for Freddy and picked him up in town. Because it was winter they were afraid that Freddy would starve or freeze to death if left to his own devices. So they fed him dinner as they spoke with him about where they might take him to stay to remain out of the cold.

Not only did Freddy refuse to leave but he barricaded himself in their bathroom and treated himself to a long shower, which was the reason for my being summoned to the scene. From the residue of dirt and grime in the shower, I could see that he had definitely need of some personal hygiene, which was to my benefit when transporting him to the county's gray bar hotel.

It took several minutes for me to talk Freddy out of the bathroom, but he refused to leave peaceably. Hence, I arrested him for trespassing and then upgraded the charge to criminal trespassing and theft when I discovered that he had pilfered some of the Good Samaritans' medications, which I recovered during my search.

On the way to the Ravalli County jail, I kept smelling an odor coming from Freddy that I couldn't quite identify, and yet it seemed familiar. After dropping him off, I contacted the couple to determine if anything else was missing from the bathroom. I knew that Freddy would drink just about anything that contained alcohol. Sure enough, the Good Samaritan found that a large bite had been taken out of his Old Spice deodorant stick. When I asked him to check the label, he said it contained alcohol as an ingredient. I had heard of people being desperate for booze, but this one took the cake—the deodorant cake.

Half of Freddy's stomach had already been removed due to the corrosive effect of alcohol. He looked like death warmed over. I pitied the couple having to clean the bathroom after him. In the coming years, I encountered Freddy many more times after he migrated to Missoula. He even tried to sue me for arresting him once again for trespassing, of all things. The case never made it to court and was dismissed due to lacking legitimate merit. I thought that sooner or later I would find Freddy dead in an alley. But, like the Energizer Bunny, he kept on going. I surmised that he was incapable of dying since he was so well preserved from freeloading so many potent spirits.

* * *

As I think about Freddy and many others I have known in the course of my vocation as a police officer, the life that God gives us is not always easy. Despite inevitable suffering, life is nonetheless a gift. Most people embrace it, some take it for granted, others use it for their own selfish gain, and still others abuse and waste it.

I spent my career dealing with the Freddy's of the world who wasted the gift of life by abusing their bodies with alcohol and drugs. I admit that often I was disgusted by them, but mostly I felt sorrowful because of their wasted lives. One of the most puzzling issues to face me as a Christian police officer is realizing how simple God's offer of salvation is, and yet wondering why some would willingly choose to reject God when he is so faithful, as he has been to my family and me. Perhaps the most crippling sin of all is living as though we belong only to ourselves and not to God.

Saint Paul wrote to the Corinthian Christians, "What? Know ye not that your body is the temple of the Holy Ghost which is in you, which ye have of God, and ye are not your own? For ye are bought with a price: therefore glorify God in your body, and in your spirit which are God's" (I Cor 6:19–20).

Yet, how often are Paul's words taken to heart?

* * *

When I arrived in Stevensville, I was initially welcomed with open arms by the citizens and town administration alike. I was even promoted to the rank of sergeant with a pay raise. Yet for the short time I was there, I was known as the infamous Sergeant Schultz. Had I taken the Hogan's Heroes' attitude of "I see nothing, I hear nothing, I do nothing," I probably would have continued to receive the good will of those surrounding me, which in my case was not to be so. Coming from my professional background in Virginia, I was more of a proactive officer than the community wanted. I didn't take the oath of office to look the other way out of political expedience.

During my tenure, I arrested a former city official and prominent business owner for a DUI, as well as some family members of city officials. I quickly fell from the community's graces and realized that mine was a job more suited for Barney Fife than for me. While Chief Lou was a good friend, he also was caught in the middle of things. So I resigned at the end of my first year. But not all was lost. For I had been given the chance to process my application with Missoula during that year. I joined the Missoula Police Department two months after resigning from Stevensville.

The year in Stevensville was one of significant learning for us as a family. Carole was living away from her family for the first time in her life, and I was far enough away from mine so that we had to depend upon one another as a married couple. We grew closer that year even though it was not always easy. More importantly, we started going to Florence Baptist Church where we became very involved as a family. While I had received Christ into my heart when I was thirteen or fourteen years old, I had not received any encouragement from my parents since they were not Christians. The people of the Florence Baptist congregation became for me that source of encouragement.

While attending Florence Baptist, my faith and the reality of my salvation made sense to me for the first time in my life. We grew as a family as we grew closer to the Lord. That closeness to Jesus was to prove so important during August of that year when we prematurely lost our son Benjamin Christopher at the seventh month of pregnancy. Benjamin was there one day during his checkup and gone the next. Carole and I had to go through the delivery process knowing, but still not believing, that we would return home from the hospital without our little boy. He was so tiny at birth, but he looked ever so perfect. His death was our first great test of faith as a couple and a family. Kristi was but three and Kimberly one. Possibly the most difficult thing for a parent to do is to explain to a very young child that the brother she was expecting would not be coming home from the hospital with mommy.

It was truly a time of deep mourning for us, but it was also a time when we leaned upon the Lord for support. Our church family was so gracious to us, as were my Uncle Herman and Aunt Marilyn Schultz and my cousins Brad and Kevin and their families.

Brad and Kevin had been the ones responsible for taking me to the meetings in which I received Christ into my life many years before. Still today, we wonder what Benjamin would have been like had he lived. At the same time, we are thankful that he is waiting in heaven to greet us on the day that we shall be ever so happy to greet him.

Weathering that storm as a couple set the stage for how we were to handle future downpours. We learned that God never promised that life would always be easy for us. He did promise, however, that he would be with us during the most difficult of times.

While living in Stevensville, I took to heart for the remainder of my life the verse of scripture that reads, "Trust in the Lord with all thine heart; and lean not unto thine own understanding. In all thy ways acknowledge him, and he shall direct thy paths" (Prov 3:5–6).

With the renewal of my faith in God's providence came a new awareness of the Holy Spirit's leading in my life.

On a morning, shortly before I resigned from the Stevensville Police Department, I felt compelled to stop by and visit with Chief Lou since he and his wife were going through a divorce that he did not want.

His wife and their daughter had recently moved out, so I wanted to know how he was doing. He was quite down that morning, so I did my best to cheer him up and remind him that no matter what might happen, God was still in control of his life. He seemed more cheery before I left and admitted that he had put his gun to his head in anticipation of ending his life that day before I arrived.

Other than offering him a few jokes and the reminder that God was his friend, I didn't drop on him any heavy words of scripture. I simply reached out to a friend whom the Holy Spirit had nudged me to visit. While I was thankful to have done so, the credit belonged to God for prompting me. Lou lived until he retired, and several more years beyond, before he passed away.

* * *

On a brighter note, Carole and I invited my brother Ken and a girl he knew to church for some special services that summer in Stevensville. At the conclusion of them, both Ken and the girl accepted Christ as their personal savior. That same weekend my brother Keith, Ken's twin, received Christ while attending a church service in Phoenix, Arizona. It was nothing short of amazing that during the same weekend, hundreds of miles apart, both of my brothers rejoiced with gratitude for their salvation. Carole and I had been praying for them, but it was God who was faithful.

CHAPTER SIX

My Dream Come True? Bombs, Bullets and Boondoggles

Who has not heard the timeless adage, "Be careful what you wish for"? My dream from nearly the first day as a young intern was to become a Missoula police officer. My goal was to be hired to work there for my entire career until retirement. I loved my city, I loved my state, and I could think of nowhere else I'd rather be, or so I thought at the time.

I learned over the next several years that observing a workplace from the outside was different from experiencing it from the inside. As far as the job was concerned, I loved it. I had heard it said that the only work to which a person could be called was the pastoral ministry. However, I can say without any shadow of a doubt that God created me and called me to be a cop. Law enforcement has been my lifetime vocation. I always looked forward to going to work to experience whatever came my way. Admittedly, I did not necessarily return home at the end of my shift feeling the same way.

My time at the Missoula Police Department was filled with good times and some not so good times, and yet, as with every place I worked, I learned and grew as a person and as a police officer.

Within days of my being hired by Missoula, I faced the loss of a brother officer, which is always one of the hardest aspects of being a cop. At 4:00 a.m., on December 4, 1984, I was awakened by a call to report immediately to the police department because a Missoula County sheriff's deputy had been shot. No other details were given. While I was driving to the station, I mentally ran through the list of deputies I knew. I first thought about Allen Kimery because I had recently attended a class at the academy with him and another deputy. We had driven together to Bozeman and back, and visited with one another during breaks from the class and at dinners. Allen was a Christian, so we had much in common. I dismissed the possibility that Allen might be the victim since I knew that he always wore his vest. But, once I arrived at the station, I discovered that I was sadly mistaken.

Sergeant Allen Kimery was just thirty-eight years old and a nine-year veteran officer as well as a military veteran. He left behind his wife Jo and two children. Jo had been our Lamaze coach for the birth of our son Benjamin and would do the same again in preparation for Melissa and Samuel.

Al was shot when he stopped a vehicle whose occupant had run off without paying for five dollars' worth of fuel from a gas station. What Al didn't know at the time was that the car had been stolen from Great Falls, Montana. Nor did he know that the suspect possessed a gun, and that, only hours before, the suspect had stated at a party that he would shoot any police officer who tried to stop him. Al had recently given his body armor, commonly referred to as a bullet resistant vest, to a new deputy on his shift. He had ordered a new one for himself, but it had not yet arrived.

My primary task was to secure the crime scene. Two city police officers had already transported Al to the emergency room a few blocks away. Sadly, the medical staff was unable to save him. I learned that the bullet had severed his aorta and that for all practical purposes he was dead the minute he was hit.

In spite of being mortally wounded, Al had displayed incredible courage and fortitude. He had emptied his .41 magnum revolver when firing at the suspect's vehicle, striking the suspect in the shoulder. As I surveyed the scene, it was most painful to view Al's life-blood spilled on the pavement. I could see just where he had gone down while attempting to regain his footing in order to get back into his patrol car in an effort to call for assistance or give pursuit. Al had a determined will to survive.

Once his car was removed from the scene, it was taken to a secure location for processing. Officer Casey Gunter and I remained as a security detail until the detectives arrived, which enabled us to return to the police station. Very shortly, we were assigned to an officer to conduct a search for the suspect's vehicle, which others soon located. It was not long before a suspicious person matching the description was spotted at a convenience store. Officers responded and took him into custody. Casey and I were at the station when they brought him in. Their professionalism was impressive, considering that each of us would have gladly taken the monster out and shot him. Yet it was not our job to dispense punishment, for that responsibility lay with the judicial system and with God.

Allen's funeral was the first of several law enforcement funerals that I attended during my career. It is always impressive to be a part of such a solemn occasion. The response of brother and sister officers from all over the country, and even Canada, is a sight to behold. With each such service I die a little death within myself in the knowledge that a brother or sister of the calling has fallen in the line of duty. We don't have to know the officers personally to be saddened, for we have walked in shoes similar to theirs, answered similar calls, and engaged in similar actions. The only difference is that we have lived to tell the stories of what happened. The attack on a police officer is an attack on our society and on every man and woman in blue.

The officers involved in the case, and Allen's family, all endured the added insult of having to sit through two court trials to obtain a conviction. Because of pre-trial publicity, both trials were held in other communities. The first ended in a hung jury because some idiot of a person on the jury had noticed a garbage dumpster in the photographs of the crime scene, near the spot where Allen had made his traffic stop.

With no evidence to substantiate her conjecture, the woman surmised that maybe, just maybe, someone had been hiding in the dumpster, waiting for a police officer to stop someone there, in order then to shoot the officer. Her reasoning was beyond absurd, because Al's fingerprints were on the suspect's vehicle and his bullet fragments in the car. Moreover, the suspect's injuries and his fingerprints were consistent with his having been in the vehicle. Even so, a hung jury was declared because no amount of logic could persuade the woman otherwise.

The tragedy was that Jo Kimery had to sit through two trials in which she was ordered not to show any emotion for fear of influencing the jury. She also had to sit stoically through presentations of the photographs of the crime scene and the autopsy of her beloved husband, not once but twice, before the suspect was convicted.

I can understand a judge not wanting a courtroom to be filled with constant screams of anguish. Yet, realistically, why shouldn't a jury be entitled to see visual evidence of the emotional turmoil experienced by the victim's family? No one wants to see an innocent person go to prison. But does that mean that juries should not get at least a glimpse of the collateral damage resulting from the murder's actions?

Al's assailant was eventually killed by another inmate during an altercation in prison, which was a small consolation, considering the life he had cut short. Allen was a friend to all who knew him. His death has left a huge hole in the Missoula law enforcement community to this very day.

Sometime later I learned that, close to the moment Al was killed, his wife Jo was awakened from her sleep by an image of Al standing at her bedside, telling her that all would be well. Was the image of Al from a dream? I cannot say. But when the knock came at her door, she had already foreknown that Al was gone.

As a Christian, I have seen that God moves in many a mysterious way, as with the miracles I have witnessed in my own life. If Jo's vision of Al was from a dream, then surely it was through that dream that God's spirit enabled Al to speak words of comfort to Jo.

* * *

As I mentioned before, I had had two primary mentors up to this stage of my career. Doug Chase had inspired me to become a police officer. His love for the job was contagious, as was borne out through his long career. Bill VanCuyck had influenced me the most when it came to how to become a good cop. Throughout all of my years in law enforcement, I utilized what Bill had taught me.

Carl Ibsen, however, was the one who likely had the greatest influence upon me as a brother officer. Carl taught me the importance of the police brotherhood and thus the meaning of honorable friendship among those who comprise the Thin Blue Line.

I met Carl when I was an intern. My earliest memory of him was of the night that a fellow officer and I were riding together, while at the same time several other officers were in pursuit of a motorcycle stolen at a house party. Carl was stationed with the Crime Attack Team in an unmarked vehicle that happened to be in the area where the pursuit ended in a collision, with the suspect bolting from the scene on foot.

While focusing his attention upon where the suspect had last been seen, Carl spotted him running down an alley. Speeding up to get abreast of him, Carl reached out the window, grabbed the suspect by the shoulder, and pulled him to a stop, at which point the suspect hollered, "I didn't steal no motorcycle."

Having heard the suspect's unsolicited confession, Carl wasted no time in identifying himself as a police officer and reading the guy his Miranda rights. Carl then arrested him on the spot. Case closed.

* * *

When I began my field training, I could not have been happier than to have Carl as my training officer. It was the start of a friendship that has weathered the ups and downs of both of us and lasted for these past thirty-eight years. Carl is more than a friend. He is my brother in Christ and my brother in blue. We don't get to see each other often, but we remain as close as if we were blood siblings.

Carl is six-foot-four and carries not an ounce of fat anywhere on his body. I learned early on that if I took him out for a meal, I'd better stock my wallet full of dollar bills. I have never met a person with his metabolism. He consumes a superabundance of calories just to maintain his weight. Secretly, I have hated him for that, because if I should so much as look at food, the process of osmosis instantly puts pounds on me. The thing that amazes me about Carl is his agility. His size-nine shoes are able to keep him aloft, defying the law of gravity.

During the first shift that I rode with Carl, I entered the passenger side of his patrol car with a small paper bag in hand that contained my lunch. He asked me what it was. When I told him, he laughed. "That's not a lunch," he said. "*This* is a lunch," as he pointed to a large gray carpenter's lunch box. As he opened it, I discovered he wasn't kidding.

When we went out together for our first coffee break, he ordered pie and ice cream. Later that night, when we pulled over for "lunch" in the area of a quarry in the South Hills of Missoula, he opened his lunch box and proceeded to devour two sandwiches, an apple, and a slice of cake, along with a thermos of coffee, while I sat quietly and ate a single sandwich. When we took the last coffee break of the shift, he ordered a full meal with desert.

Needless to say, over the course of the next few weeks of field training I took more than a little razzing from him. It just so happened that at that very same time, Saturday Night Live featured the Cone Heads, a group of aliens often consuming mass quantities of food.

Naw, I thought. It couldn't be, could it? Was Carl was one of them?

Regardless, he was a freak of nature, absent the cone-shaped head.

One of the funniest stories about training with Carl took place on Higgins Avenue in downtown Missoula. The North end of Higgins merged into a circle near the old train depot affectionately known as "the drag," where in those days teenagers hung out to cruise.

One night, while we were sitting at a stop light, a teenage girl's car rear-ended us. As we worked the accident and prepared the paperwork for the police report, she sat in the back seat of our patrol car, thoroughly inconsolable.

Attempting to lighten up the situation, Carl looked at her birthdate and commented, "I was headed to Vietnam when you were born." But his remark was to no avail.

As he continued trying to calm her down, she repeatedly said, "My dad is going to kill me."

Finally Carl retorted, "Look, miss, I've been doing this job for a number of years now, and I've yet to see a father kill his daughter over a minor traffic accident."

Still she persisted. "You just don't understand!"

Carl replied, "What don't I understand?"

She said, "This is the second accident I've had this week, and the first car I hit was a Highway Patrol car."

What were the odds?

Carl and I glanced at one another, trying not to laugh. Then Carl looked at her and said, "Well, you might just be the first!"

* * *

At the end of my field training, Carl passed me with flying colors. Once more, I was on my own. To say that the next few years were interesting would be to say the least.

When one thinks of Missoula, Montana, the tendency is to think of it as a remote and peaceful little western town. In actuality, when I went to work in Missoula it was the third largest city in the state. In the years to come it grew to the second largest. When comparing the city's number of police officers to the size of its population, our department received proportionately the same percentage of calls as the departments of larger cities.

Additionally, Missoula is the major trade center for the four surrounding counties. The main difference between Missoula and the rest of Montana's larger cities is that a greater number of gun owners reside in Missoula due to its hunting heritage, as a result of which I never worried much about the guns people told me about.

Rather, I worried more about the guns they didn't tell me about. In fact, I stopped more vehicles with rifles hung on back window racks than I can possibly count.

During my departmental training, I had the joy of attending my first autopsy, conducted on the cadaver of a man killed in a hunting accident. By a long shot (no pun intended), autopsies were not the worst things I saw as a cop who had no desire to attend them. While necessary for obtaining forensic evidence, autopsies weren't the highlight of my day.

One afternoon on day shift in the spring of 1985, I was working radar in one of our local neighborhoods from which the department had received a number of speeding complaints. After ticketing several vehicles, I stopped a lady with her children in the back seat. She was cordial but appeared stressed. While I checked her driver's license, her vehicle registration, and her proof of insurance, I noted that all three had expired. As I pointed this out, she began crying profusely.

Normally, I did not let tears stop me from writing a ticket, because I had learned that women will sometimes use their emotions to gain sympathy, hoping to get out of a citation. While I do not think of myself as sexist, and hold no grudges against women, it is a fact that I and most police officers have learned through experience.

In this instance, however, I sensed that there was more to the story, for she was sincerely distraught. I asked her why she had allowed her license, registration, and insurance to elapse. She replied through her tears that her husband had always taken care of those things. So I enquired as to why he had not done so this time. She said that he had been killed in a hunting accident the previous fall. It was then that her last name clicked in my head. She was the wife of the man whose autopsy I had attended months earlier. I suppose you could say that a wayward shot carries a long distance for a long time in a small town.

At that point I fought back my own tears and did something I rarely did. After explaining to her how to handle all of the official matters that needed attention, I let her go with only a warning. Then, after getting back into my patrol car, I must admit, I shed more than a few tears in empathy with the grief that she and her children were enduring.

Believe it or not, cops can be, and usually are, very compassionate people. While I made every attempt to enforce the law fairly and equitably, I learned that sometimes a compassionate warning served the same or better purpose than a citation. In that respect, a passage from Philippians comes to mind.

> *If there be therefore any consolation in Christ, if any comfort of love, if any fellowship of the Spirit, if any bowels and mercies, Fulfill ye my joy, that ye be likeminded, having the same love, being of one accord, of one mind. Let nothing be done through strife or vainglory; but in lowliness of mind let each esteem other better than themselves. Look not every man on his own things, but every man also on the things of others. Let this mind be in you, which was also in Christ Jesus.* (Phil 2:1–5)

During her husband's autopsy I learned that he probably could have lived. He was accidentally shot by his hunting partner when taking aim at an elk. The partner did not realize that his friend was on the opposite side of the draw in the woods that the two were hunting. When the partner fired, he missed the elk and hit his friend. The partner applied a tourniquet to his friend's leg and then hiked out of the woods for help. The victim at some point released the tourniquet, either out of intense pain or because he feared the possibility of living without a leg.

Only God knows just what happened there at the end, and why an elk's life was spared, and why a grieving widow and her fatherless children were found by a policeman who, having seen for himself her husband's mortal wound, simply could not hold back his own tears.

In such a time, if there be any consolation, any comfort of love, and any fellowship of the Spirit, then surely it is the "consolation in Christ" who, suffering as we suffer and dying as we die, gives us life.

* * *

Some officers don't like working vehicular traffic because they believe it prevents them from taking the emergency radio calls that they frequently prefer. In police vernacular, I suppose it could be said that I was a tail-light chaser, meaning that I enjoyed working the traffic because of the public contacts I made. I believed that I might be saving lives, especially in those areas where high numbers of accidents occurred.

More importantly, Bill VanCuyk taught me that people who commit crimes also drive cars. He believed that an observant officer working the traffic would make more "collars" (arrests) than solely by issuing traffic tickets. During my career I made thousands of traffic stops, which yielded numerous warrant arrests, drug arrests, the arrest of several fugitives, and any number of other arrests for felonies and misdemeanors.

While working a late-night shift in the dead of winter, I came upon a vehicle that veered left and then right, coming close to hitting cars on both sides of the street. I feared that I could not stop it before it caused an accident. Luckily, the driver responded to my flashing lights and pulled over. As I approached her side of the car, she opened her window and out poured a fog of pot smoke. Not only was she high, but she couldn't see for all the smoke. And I suddenly had flashback to the old Cheech and Chong movies I had seen as a teenager.

She miserably failed the field sobriety maneuvers, so I placed her in my car. She told me the dope she had been smoking was her boyfriend's. When I pulled him out of the car, I discovered that he had no identification on him. He gave me a name and date of birth. But when I processed the name through the computer, no such name came back as being on file.

Mr. Doe, as we shall call him, had already given me permission to search the car, where I found the marijuana they had been smoking, along with a small baggy. I arrested Mr. Doe on a misdemeanor charge of drug possession.

Once we got to the station, I spoke in greater depth with the girlfriend. She gave me Mr. Doe's real name and said that she had met him only a couple of months before, and that he was from Hawaii. She added that she wondered why anyone would leave Hawaii for a cold Montana winter.

When I confronted Mr. Doe, he sighed and admitted that he had lied. His reason for lying? Hawaii had issued a fugitive warrant for his arrest, for felony possession and trafficking in cocaine.

A police officer's working of vehicular traffic invariably pays off when it comes to putting a stop to other forms of trafficking.

* * *

Among my peers I was considered to be a DUI hound. Missoula had lost an officer in 1982, due to a drunk driver having run a stop sign. I had known Officer Stephen LePiane before he had been a police officer. He was a serving a college internship while I was serving my high school internship at the same time. He went on to join the Missoula Police Department after college while I went into the ARMY after high school.

Steve was a high-energy person who liked to be in the thick of things. He was killed while backing up a fellow officer on a traffic stop when the drunk driver blew a stop sign at a high rate of speed. Although Steve was wearing his seatbelt, he was thrown violently from his patrol car into a vehicle parked along the front line of a car dealership. He hit with such force that the imprint of his badge was embedded on the vehicle's hood.

I was unable to attend Steve's funeral because I was in the military at that time. On one of my leaves home before his death, he and I had had a great time catching up as I rode along with him during one of his shifts. And even though I was away from Missoula when Steve died, his death left me with a burning desire to get drunks off the road.

Through the years I arrested somewhere in the neighborhood of 300 drivers for DUIs. While working DUI team details, I processed several hundred more. Our city and county attorneys' offices considered me an expert witness for DUI arrests. I believe to this day that my efforts likely saved many lives, just as other officers had whenever they removed drunk drivers from the road.

On Christmas Eve one year, I was dispatched to a traffic accident at a car dealership. A truck had jumped the curb and nearly run into the show room. When I arrived, the driver, an elderly gentleman, was still behind the wheel. Old MacDonald (not his real name) was quite inebriated. After he miserably failed the field sobriety maneuvers, I placed him under arrest for a DUI.

He had not provided me with his driver's license when he gave me his other paperwork. So once we were in the car and headed for the station, I once again asked Mac for his driver's license, to which he replied that he did not have one. When I asked why not, he said, "I never saw the need for it."

With Old Mac being in his seventies, I was taken aback by his remark. So I asked if he had ever gotten a ticket for not having a driver's license. He admitted that he had received one back in 1935, and had paid the fine for the infraction. But he figured he still didn't need a drivers license either then or now because he already knew how to drive. "I'm just an old farmer and I rarely drive to town," he told me. A DUI was one of the few charges for which I didn't give breaks to drivers over the holidays.

At the conclusion of the booking process at the station, Mac opted to call his wife to pick him up. It was apparent by the conversation that Mrs. MacDonald was not a happy camper. Mac was over six feet tall and still in reasonably good shape from working the farm all his life.

When Mrs. MacDonald arrived, she was every bit of five-foot nothing. She barely came up to his chest. But oh, what a little spitfire! She chewed Mac up one side and down the other for missing Christmas Eve with their kids, grandkids, and great grandkids.

As they walked out of the station, she literally took hold of him by an ear and led his by-now stooped body out to the parking lot. He must have pled guilty to the charge because his case never went to trial. I later enquired at the courthouse to verify that, yes, he had in fact finally gotten a driver's license. Whatever penalty the court imposed on him I am certain paled in comparison to the wrath of Mrs. Mac. I felt sorry for the old fella, but not sorry enough to let him off the hook for a DUI.

* * *

I witnessed many other antics while processing drunk drivers. On one occasion I was processing a young cowboy. When I asked him how much he had had to drink that night, he reached into his shirt pocket and pulled out a dozen beer tabs and began counting them.

On yet another night, I asked a fella I was processing for a DUI what he was doing prior to being arrested. He replied, "I was sleeping with the judges wife." This would have been the same judge who was to hear his case, and whose wife was homebound. So his answer didn't hold any water.

Suffice it to say that neither of these cases went to court. But I wish I could have been a fly on the wall, had they tried to hire an attorney.

Late one night, I was in a pursuit of a suspect who had attempted to run away because of outstanding warrants against him. I shall refer to this young lad as Mr. Almost, on account of the fact that he almost got away.

Mr. Almost abandoned his car at the fence line of the local public golf course and was scaling the chain link fence as I skidded to a stop. As he went over the top, I nosed my patrol car up to the fence, jumped out of the car, leapt onto the hood and launched myself upward towards the top of the fence.

It was precisely at that moment that I realized that there was an electric strand of wire along the fence top. Believe me when I say that I tried, but as a mere mortal in thin air it was impossible to reverse my momentum. I was prepared to be shocked as I grabbed the top rail of the fence. Never had I been so thankful that someone had forgotten to turn on the electricity.

If anyone were to wonder just how this chubby little police officer *thought* he would be able to leap over that fence, it's because I was not quite so portly in my younger days.

Mr. Almost had a good run, and so did several other police officers chasing after him until he was captured.

* * *

As long as I live, I will never understand the thinking process of judges. Most are pretty sharp, but every once in a while that is not so.

On Front Street in downtown Missoula there stood a tire store that was alarmed against fire and burglary. It was not one of those systems that trips the alarm every time a leaf blows by. It was an honest-to-good one that actually worked. Occasionally a large bird set it off, but it was at least ninety-percent accurate. So whenever we received the alarm, we would salivate like a dog chasing a bone. And that was because we knew that a criminal was about to go to jail.

On this particular night we arrived to see the suspect climbing over the back fence. As we descended upon him, he realized that his only escape route was by swimming across the cold Clark Fork River. As I recall, it was early spring and the water none to warm. My shift partners and I were trained not to do stupid things like jumping into a cold river at night to chase Bert the Burglar. We did what any responsible, self-respecting officer would do. We used that modern piece of technology called the radio to position additional officers on the other side of the river.

While the idea was good on paper, it did not quite measure up to plan. Bert made it across the river ahead of our units and ran into an abandoned sawmill. Being a relatively quiet weeknight, most of the shift responded to the "Y'all, come" party.

Within the next several minutes, Bert popped up in different locations like Peter Rabbit, and the chase was on. We thought we had finally cornered him in the Loyola Rams high school football field. But he popped up and ran again, so I gave chase across the field as Bert refused to heed my orders to halt.

Since we were rapidly approaching a fence next to the woods just beyond us, I did the only logical thing that a cop would do when carrying a large multi-cell Maglite. I winged the Maglite at him like a football. I was never much of a football player, but for once this aspiring quarterback threw a perfectly complete pass delivered right between Bert's shoulder blades. He was just beginning to climb the fence on the opposite side of the field when the Maglite connected with a mighty thwack! And Bert went down like a 140-pound running back who had been clothes-lined by a 300-pound lineman, which took his desire to flee right out of him.

I say all of this to point out a bizarre judgment made by the judge the next morning at arraignment. According to the detectives, Bert had already admitted to seventeen burglaries (all felonies) after his arrest. Given those, plus the fiasco of the night before, the judge in his infinite wisdom decided that Bert was not a flight risk.

Now, I don't purport to be the brightest tack in the box, but hadn't we all just spent the night chasing Bert because he was fleeing? According to the judge, not a flight risk?

Ponder on that thought for a while. The judge's reasoning was that Bert had been a long-time resident of the community.

* * *

During Easter weekend I was training a new rookie when a Pontiac Firebird came screaming by us on South Brooks Street, driving recklessly. We didn't have time to switch places, so I let the rookie drive the patrol car. All and all, he did a good job staying with the suspect's vehicle on the curves, turns, and short streets, but the Firebird walked away from us on the strait stretches.

The pursuit continued for several minutes before ending when the suspect turned off all his lights and disappeared out of our sight before turning into a neighborhood apartment complex. One of my partners found the vehicle a short time later. The suspect was long gone. Prior to towing the vehicle, I conducted an inventory of the car. Resting on the console was a furlough slip belonging to a prisoner from the Montana State Prison.

I had no idea that prisoners could get furloughs, but here it was in black and white, permitting No Luck Jones to visit his mother for Easter because she was sick with cancer.

Imagine. No Luck Jones was out partying when he should have been spending time with his dear old mom. If an award had been given for best son of the year, then No Luck would not have been in contention. No Luck had left a number of empties as well as an open containers of alcohol in the car, irrespective of the fact that his furlough stated that there was to be no alcohol consumption.

After clearing the scene, we went to No Luck's house in an effort to locate him. We spoke to his mother who said that he had not yet come home. I told her I would need to speak with No Luck tomorrow evening, and asked her to make sure that he came to the station by 10 P.M. Sure enough, No Luck showed up at the requested time. Of course, he denied any knowledge of a pursuit. But after showing him the furlough paper, he decided that it might be in his best interest to come forth with an accurate story. He was due to be released from prison in three months, that is, until he racked up another fifteen months from all of the charges.

The No Luck story is amusing, but the car he was driving made it even more so. The Firebird had been taken as collateral for a bond posted by another man. It was then lent to a friend of the bondsman who promptly lent it to another friend. And that friend lent it to No Luck.

Had it not been for No Luck's diligence in leaving us a trail of bread-crumbs, or, I should say, his furlough paper, then there was little likelihood we ever would have caught him. Some people simply are not cut out to be criminals, or at least smart ones. We can only hope that No Luck learned his lesson. But then, who would bet on it?

* * *

One of the cool things about TV cops is watching them kick doors down. My first go at it did not end well. While I was chasing a fleeing suspect down a hall at the old Palace Hotel, he ran into a room and slammed the door and locked it just as I reached it.

This was my first chance to play T.J. Hooker, an old eighties TV cop played by William Shatner.

I promptly stepped back, cocked my right leg, and kicked with all the oomph I could muster. It was an epic effort . . . right up to the point where my boot connected with the hollow core of the door. A moment that should have been pure euphoria quickly turned into shock and embarrassment, for the door remained locked with my leg firmly ensconced in it.

If you know anything about hollow core doors, they cave inward with force and then fold back in splinters as you pull your foot out. The bad guy patiently awaited his arrest while being engulfed in laughter as my partners forced the door open with my leg still stuck firmly in it. Multitudes of wood slivers were embedded in my leg and pants when I extricated myself from the trap.

My luck with doors did not improve much over the years. The next episode came right out of the Keystone Cops. When Montana enacted its domestic violence laws, it required the police to make a short statement to the offender before making an arrest. We had to state that once we were dispatched to the scene of a domestic incident and determined that physical violence had occurred, we were then obligated by law to arrest the offender, prefacing the arrest with the statement, "You are under arrest." As you might imagine, this often presented problems.

Sergeant Steve Ross and Officer Dean Bohnsack and I responded to a domestic disturbance one evening. Upon our arrival we met the victim at a neighbor's house. She had injuries on her face and neck consistent with an assault, and advised us that her husband had been the assailant. She stated that he was volatile and had weapons in the house. So the three of us went to the front door and knocked. The suspect, whom I'll refer to as Mr. He-Man-Wife-Beater, answered the door. He was visibly upset and admitted that he had had an altercation with his wife. Things went pretty well right up to the point that I advised him he was under arrest.

Mr. He-Man was a walking advertisement for a weightlifting gym. He sought to shut the door in our faces. Fearing that he would go for a weapon, all three of us hit the door at the same time. We must have eaten our Wheaties that morning because down came the door with the frame attached, with Mr. He-man beneath the door, and all three of us on top of him. If someone had had a camera, we could have won a fortune on the Funniest Home Videos show.

But we were immediately faced with a dilemma. How were we gracefully to detach ourselves from the door and from each other and then remove the door from Mr. He-Man who was none too happy or cooperative?

Once having slid the door and the frame aside, the fight was on. Mr. He-Man's arms were as thick as my thigh and he was none too eager to relinquish them to my handcuffs. I managed to get one of them on one wrist while we struggled with the other. Unfortunately, just as we raised the other wrist, I came down with the second cuff with such momentum that before Officer Bohnsack could move his thumb out of the way, the force of the cuff had hammered Mr. He-Man's wrist and nearly detached Officer Bohnsack's thumb in what we refer to as a closed, traumatic amputation.

Shortly after Officer Bohnsack returned to work after recovering from his surgery that winter, he slid on the ice during a call and hit the same wrist on a car bumper. The only way to fix it that time was to fuse his wrist and his thumb. What had begun as a Keystone Cops comedy routine quickly turned into a tragedy that ended Officer Dean Bohnsack's career. I apologized to Dean on more than one occasion. And while he forgave me, I cannot help but feel guilty even now.

Needless to say, the incident added a number of additional charges to Mr. He-Man-Wife-Beater's criminal resume.

* * *

My next "door debacle" occurred during another domestic beef. My partner Brian Damaskos and I arrived at the location and approached the house. From inside we could hear a woman screaming. Brian went to the back door while I went to the front.

I knocked loudly and announced my presence. The woman's screaming was persuasive enough for me to believe that she was about to be killed. So I did what any red-blooded police officer would do. I kicked in the door, successfully, I might add, and with it only half of the door frame this time. As I entered with my weapon drawn, the door swung around and smacked the wall. I stepped into the house, only to see Officer Damaskos walking unimpeded through the unlocked back door. Indeed, the couple was arguing vociferously. Yet no one was being killed, and no one had cuts or bruises indicating that the dispute had turned physical. So they rapidly earned the distinction of being known as Mr. & Mrs. Cry Wolf. Mrs. Wolf simply wanted to make the point that Mr. Wolf should not have spoken to her in the manner in which he did.

After determining that the only peace they had disturbed was their own, we cleared the scene. I then called my shift supervisor to advise that the city might be paying for a new door, a new lock, and a new frame. My luck with doors still hadn't changed.

When I met with my supervisor and explained the situation, I noticed that the city's mayor was riding along with him that night. I thought to myself, So much then for my staying under the radar. Thankfully, Mr. and Mrs. Cry Wolf apparently made the repairs on their own, sparing me of the embarrassment of having to explain to the city manager the state of the door, the lock, and the frame and why he had to pay for them.

* * *

Early one Sunday evening, my shift Lieutenant Russ Pulliam and I were dispatched to a serious accident on Interstate 90 between Russell and Orange Streets. The situation would normally have been handled by the Montana Highway Patrol. But because their officers were out of position, Russ and I were called to respond. Russ arrived first and I came shortly behind him.

When I pulled up, I could see that Russ was attending a victim lying on the roadway. The demolished car was off to the side on the shoulder.

As I rushed to the lieutenant's aid, thinking he was about to begin first aid, he warned me to watch my step. He had just turned the victim over to check the victim's pulse. Through what had been the victim's eye sockets we could now see only the pavement. Glancing around, I realized that I was walking through a minefield of human body parts. The victim, of course, was deceased. There was nothing we could do except to secure the scene and await the Highway Patrol. As a result of the victim's multiple injuries, the body was unidentifiable as either male or female. The car's registration indicated, however, that it belonged to a girl who had attended grade school and high school with me. Her identity was confirmed the following day.

She had not been restrained by her seatbelt, and was partially ejected during the crash and landed beneath the car's roof as it skidded down the interstate, grinding her to pieces.

I had not been close to the victim in the past, but I remembered how she looked before the accident, and felt a terrific stab of anguish for her family. As difficult as it was for me to see what little remained of her, I preferred to be the one, rather than a family member or friend, to deal with the visual horror of that moment.

Memories of her have long since been filed away in the back of my mind. Yet they are impossible to forget, for now and then they resurface with a tinge of that same stab of anguish.

* * *

On a lighter note, one night the Highway Patrol was in pursuit of a vehicle heading from the airport to the city. I happened to be located nearby at the city fuel pumps from which I was able to pull in behind the suspect as he passed me. The Highway Patrol officer was about a quarter of a mile back. The suspect, whom we shall call Mr. Louie DUI, veered into an industrial park and stopped when he realized there was nowhere else for him to go. I pulled up behind him and waited a minute for the Highway Patrol officer to catch up with me.

Together we approached the vehicle. As the patrol officer ordered Louie out of the car, I approached from the passenger side. I could see that the passenger was a female who appeared to be wearing a strange outfit with highly pronounced, pointed shoulders, not unlike space suits seen in science fiction movies of the fifties and sixties.

Mr. Louie DUI was so intoxicated that he was unable to perform any of the sobriety maneuvers safely. The patrol officer arrested him and requested that I standby for someone to retrieve the vehicle or tow it away. So I asked Space Girl to step out of the car, and enquired as to who might come to get the car since the driver was being arrested for driving under the influence.

Space Girl advised me that she would be happy to drive the vehicle home. But Space Girl was obviously intoxicated herself. So I advised against it. Yet she reiterated that she was perfectly capable of driving. So once again I advised her that I did not believe she was sober enough.

By this time Space Girl was utterly frustrated with me and continued to insist. So I asked her, "Miss, are you sure you are capable of driving when you are standing here talking to me with your dress inside out?"

She looked at herself and sheepishly admitted that I was probably right. The only person she could think of, who might come to drive the vehicle, was a fellow I had arrested the week before for driving on a suspended license. He was definitely a no-go. So I called for a tow truck and gave the poor embarrassed Space Girl a ride home.

Not only was her dress inside out, which accounted for the shoulder boards looking like wings on a space suit, but the dress was buttoned up crookedly. I figured that it must have been quite a feat for her to put on that dress while all of her lingerie lay in the back seat as Mr. Louie DUI gunned the car away from the Highway Patrol.

Since Mr Louie DUI was fully clothed, we leave the remainder of the story to the imagination.

* * *

Our SWAT team was called out one afternoon to deal with a suspect barricaded at the old Palace Hotel. I was stationed on the perimeter when I was instructed to take some equipment to the command post.

Unfortunately, the officer instructing me did not give clear directions as to the route I should take, nor did he pinpoint the exact location of the suspect. As I carried the equipment to the rear of the hotel, for a few seconds I was exposed to the shooter, which was just enough time for him to fire a shot that hit near my feet and considerably expedited my race to safety. I felt like that poor fella caught in the middle of the street in a Hollywood western with a gunslinging bully firing at his feet, telling him to dance. Just so, I took an indirect route of return to my car at the conclusion of the mission.

Domestic disturbances always have the potential for becoming dangerous situations for the officers who respond to them. More than once I have been attacked by Mama once she saw Papa being handcuffed for spousal abuse. For, once the provider of the paycheck goes out the door, the abused person often forgets about the beatings endured.

One Sunday afternoon I rolled up on a domestic disturbance in progress within the circle at the end of Higgins Avenue, near the old train station. I was just approaching when I observed a man knocking his wife down with a "haymaker." I had barely made the call for backup when the fight was on.

As I took the man to the ground, the woman jumped on my back and took a wild swing at me. It was the first and thankfully last time that I became a cop sandwich! A Good Samaritan on a bicycle stopped and jumped into the fray to help me. We restrained both suspects before my backup arrived. Things could have gotten much uglier had the good citizen not assisted. Given some of the current attitudes towards police, I fear that an officer in a similar situation today may not be so lucky.

* * *

One time during an evening shift, I responded to a disturbance in a downstairs apartment from which I could hear a woman screaming. My zone partner, Officer Mark Horner, and I descended the stairs to the apartment after entering by the unlocked upstair's door. At the base of the steps a man was locking his arm around the neck of a woman as he held a chair leg in his opposite hand, threatening to beat her, or beat us, should we get any closer.

For the next fifteen minutes I talked with the suspect, seeking to persuade him to release the woman and come upstairs with us. He finally agreed to do so and to put down the chair leg, provided that we backed ourselves up the stairs first. He still had his arm around the woman's throat.

When at last we all reached the top of the steps, Mark and I pulled the woman away from the man to safety as the man quickly dashed back down the steps.

I followed him as he ran into the kitchen where he grabbed a knife. As he started to round the kitchen counter towards me, I drew my weapon and told him that I would shoot if he came any closer. It took another ten minutes of talking him down before he finally dropped the knife. We took him into custody without further incident.

It was only when we handcuffed him that I discovered he was holding a standard dinner knife that I had previously been unable to identify as such due to poor lighting. Of course, even a dinner knife can cause significant injury or death.

As the minutes passed during those tense moments, I seriously thought that I might have to take his life. I was prepared to do so if necessary, but it was the last thing I wanted. He later asked me if indeed I would have shot him. I assured him that I would have done so if he had further threatened my partner or me.

To this day, I doubt that the guy knew just how close he came to dying. And I thank God that I didn't have to take his life because of a dinner knife that was meant for slicing beef or butter but definitely not my hide.

* * *

Calls involving children are among the cases that police officers dread the most. I was dispatched one afternoon for a welfare check on a woman and her two boys. She and her husband had been going through a nasty divorce and were engaged in a custody dispute. The father had requested officers to conduct a welfare check on his kids, because the mother had made veiled threats, saying that if she could not take possession of the children then no one would.

When I arrived at the house, no one responded to my knocks on the door and the announcement of my presence. I decided to peer through the windows for signs of anything being amiss. As I rounded the back of the house I noticed a detached garage. From its interior I could hear the sound of an engine running.

With the side door locked, and the main door pulled down and locked, the garage was filled with exhaust smoke.

Through the glass I could see a female slumped behind the wheel. With the aid of the fire department now on scene we gained access to the garage. The wife was already deceased from carbon monoxide poisoning. The two small children lay beneath her body, showing advanced signs of asphyxiation from the fumes. Both were transported by ambulance to the hospital where they succumbed to carbon monoxide poisoning later that night.

The inhumanity of people, especially in relation to their children, is so very difficult to understand. My heart ached for the father. I could not withhold my tears as I thought of my own children being of approximately the same age, safely at home. I am ashamed to admit, even now, that my anger towards the mother still wells up within me because of her thoroughly selfish act, killing her children to her spite her husband. All too frequently children become pawns in the hands of parents who should protect them and not abuse them for nefarious purposes.

The Bible is replete with examples of human depravity, as far back as Cain's slaughter of his brother Abel (Gen 4:1–16), all the way through to the moment when Judas Iscariot traitorously betrayed Jesus for thirty pieces of silver, which precipitated Christ's death (Mark 14:43–46).

I will never understand this world's open rebellion against God and his son Jesus, our savior. God's salvation is available to all who repent and seek God's forgiveness in personal relationship and response to him. "If the Son therefore shall make you free, ye shall be free indeed" (John 8:36).

Oh, if only more people were to wake up free—free for their own sake, and free for the sake of their children.

***

After walking the beat one night my partner and I went back to the station to pick up our patrol cars for the remainder of the shift. I had driven barely a block away from the station when I heard a loud explosion coming from the direction I had just left.

Along with other units I arrived at the station and discovered that someone had placed a bomb beneath one of our unmarked patrol cars. My beat partner and I had just walked past the car and then driven back by it only minutes before it exploded. We were extremely fortunate that the bomb didn't detonate sooner than it did.

The suspect was later apprehended. He worked as a cook for a local restaurant frequented by other cops in the area as well as by me. It turned out that the man was on parole, that he hated cops, and that he had been spitting in our food as he cooked it. I have often wondered if perhaps I was one of the misfortunate souls to have ingested his spittle. Ignorance is bliss I guess.

Officer discretion can be fun at times. Case in point was the night I was patrolling through downtown Missoula when I observed four young miscreants in a parking lot behind a row of closed businesses. I requested an additional unit to back me up. As we approached the youths they ran. My partner went one way and caught two of the boys, while I took off after another who ran across the parking lot towards the river.

I pulled up my patrol car next to him, jumped out, and grabbed him. As I swung him around onto the hood of my patrol car, he landed with a thud and cracking sound. I had the frightening thought that maybe I had broken some of the kid's ribs. Glancing at the hood and windshield, I noticed that they were covered with a clear, gooey, yellowish substance. As it was, the teen was carrying nearly an entire carton of eggs stuffed inside his jacket. When I questioned all of them as to what they had been doing, they admitted to egging cars at a local senior living residence a short distance away on Orange Street.

I confess that I am not a big fan of what today is called restorative justice, because all too often it doesn't work. Like an alcoholic in recovery, a delinquent must want to change before change is possible. However, I saw an opportunity to teach them a lesson that I hoped would last a lifetime.

Once I got to the station, I called and spoke with the parents of the three stooges and presented my plan. I could either routinely cite them to juvenile court for criminal mischief or we could handle the matter my way. The parents readily agreed to handling it my way.

With that, I drove "Larry, Curly, and Moe" to the Super America Station on the corner of the street down from the senior center. Having borrowed a bucket and bought some soap and cotton cloths, I took my newly designated teen-comedy team to the senior living center where, at the wee hour of 2:30 a.m., they washed each and every car they had egged. Once all of the vehicles were as clean as possible under the canopy of darkness, I called the parents to come and pick up their not-so-hardened criminals. I then asked the parents to escort their kids to the senior center in the morning to apologize personally to all of the victims whose names I had obtained by checking the cars' license registrations. The boys were then to wash each car once more to the owner's satisfaction.

All three parents called the station the following evening to give a report. They said that "Larry, Curly and Moe" were completely humbled by the experience and swore off of their lives of crime, which were not worthy of them. Frankly, I wondered if my efforts had really done much good.

Several months later, I was talking with my sister Connie and learned that she was a friend of one of the mothers. Recently the two had met and my name had come up in the conversation. The mother said to Connie that the experience had been the best thing that had ever happened to her son. He came away from it with a newly found respect for both cops and other people, which led me to believe that sometimes we cops really do make a difference—the difference between a life of crime and a life lived as God intends it to be.

* * *

Regrettably, however, there are some people who seem born to spend their lives in prison. When they are released, it seems they can't get back to prison quickly enough.

Such was the case with a fellow I'll call Mr. Jail Bird, or J.B. for short. As for the extent of his criminal life a string of burglaries occurred over the course of several weeks one fall and winter. What was strange about them was that nearly all of the burglaries took place at a location named Professional Village. The situation got to a point that all of us on the late night shift who worked the area became thoroughly irritated with being called to deal with the various hits, often at the same business previously hit. We couldn't help but take it personally. We tried stakeouts to catch the suspect. We walked the complex several times each night, shaking doors. More than once we received a call about a burglary in progress minutes after we left. The call was always anonymous, so we believed it was the perpetrator calling in to taunt us. Our efforts at tracking the caller were to no avail.

One night during a freshly fallen snow we received the dreaded call. By this time, any nearby officers would habitually flock to the area, flood the streets, and look for suspects.

Officer Willy Reed found some fresh bicycle tracks on the sidewalk. Seeing where the bicycle had been hidden behind some bushes, he followed the tracks to a house several blocks away just off of the Orange Street Bridge. At last, we believed, we had found our man, J.B.

We conducted a search of the house, and not only did we find evidence of his crimes, but we also located a stack of pornographic magazines that J.B. had already forwarded under his own name to the Montana State Penitentiary. When interviewing J.B., who was out on parole, he readily admitted to the crimes.

We asked him why he had kept burglarizing the same locations. He said that, while the place was called the "Professional" Village, its people really were not professional at all. For each time he returned he realized they had taken no measures to thwart yet another crime, nor had they changed the locations where they stored their money and other valuables.

We asked him if any of our officers had ever come close to catching him. He said that he had actually held the door shut so it wouldn't open while we shook it. Learning this fact gave us the willies. I wondered if I had ever been one of the officers shaking the door.

When we asked him if he was the anonymous caller who had repeatedly called 911, he admitted to that too. His motivation, he said, was that he greatly enjoyed the sight of our pretty police lights flashing past him across the bridge by night.

For his unparalleled efforts, J.B. happily received an all-expenses-paid excursion back to the Montana State Prison.

* * *

Another person, who was not an especially humorous soul, was also destined to be a prison "lifer." I received a dispatch to a local bar and grill early one evening, concerning the report of a sexual assault involving a minor. When I arrived I was met by the father of the young boy who had been assaulted in the establishment's restroom by a middle-age male adult.

The suspect was still present. I was amazed that the father was able to show the restraint that he did. While one of my partners detained the suspect, I interviewed the nine-year-old victim who gave details of the assault.

Once I completed my interview with the boy, I placed the suspect under arrest and escorted him to my patrol car where I read him his Miranda rights and questioned him about the crime. He corroborated everything the boy had told me.

When I questioned him further, he stated that he had just been released from the Montana State Prison the day before, having served a long sentence for similar assaults. He said that he simply couldn't make it on the outside and knew he would re-offend. He believed the best way to live was to go back to prison. Thankfully, the court system obliged and sent him back to where he belonged. Some people are apparently beyond rehabilitation. Sadly, it took the victimization of a young boy to drive home the point.

* * *

Most cops are notorious practical jokers, which is an important avenue for combatting the stress of the job.

I sat one evening at Ruby's Café in Missoula, having my dinner with one of my partners. The department used fleet keys at the time, which often came in handy if you needed to get into another officers patrol car during a call. But fleet keys could also be used for villainous purposes. Upon returning to my patrol car, I discovered that a horrific crime had been committed against me. Junior had been kidnapped from my patrol car.

Before anyone accuses me of being an unfit parent for having left Junior in the car while I ate my meal, allow me to explain. Junior had been my silent sidekick ever since I had joined the department. Junior was about sixteen inches tall, eighteen inches long, and roughly twelve inches wide. He was gray and red in color and carried everything I would ever need for doing my job, including departmental forms, a finger-printing kit, extra bullets, hobble (should I need it to rope a horse or gangster), and assorted other important items. Junior was my trusty old bag, affectionately named such by some of my partners in the department. Needless to say, they would kid me about Junior. But guess who they called when they needed a form or a piece of equipment! Why, of course, they sought to borrow it from Junior.

On that fateful night, I discovered a note attached to my steering wheel. The note was written on paper and applied with tape removed from Junior's innards. Personally, I felt violated, and I couldn't imagine how Junior must have felt. The note read: "If you ever want to see Junior alive again, don't call the cops." Considering that I was a cop, I presumed this meant I could not even call myself.

The note further instructed me to follow the directions it provided. Not wanting to create a general panic in the community, I dutifully followed the instructions. The note led me to another location and note, and to yet another item ripped from poor Junior's bowels. The situation persisted for several minutes as I was directed from place to place, all the while trying to find my lost buddy. My hopes of a good outcome diminished with each new element of Junior's guts that I found dispersed around town like discarded trash. My worst fears came true when I stood at the commode in the mayor's office in city hall. For there I found Junior to be a mere shell of himself, along with a Baby Ruth candy bar perched on top that the perpetrator had left behind.

Later, on my way out the door of the police station, with Junior once again intact, I discovered two crime-scene photos that were apparently taken by an accomplice who had casually placed them in plain view for my indulgence. I eventually identified the perpetrator whom I nicknamed Officer Sticky Fingers. The pain and misery I suffered over the savaging of poor Junior was almost too great to bear, once I realized that the culprit was a fellow officer. Had he no shame or pity? Apparently not.

Sticky Fingers was duly tried and convicted by a court of his peers. To make amends for his crime, his punishment was to take me out for a cup of coffee.

And who, would you guess, received a call the next time Sticky Fingers needed a form to fill out?

You guessed it.

None other than Junior.

* * *

The good Lord has a way of humbling rookies as well as veteran police officers. Just about the time you think you've gotten it all together and you're flying high, you encounter one of those moments that brings you down to earth.

Such was the occasion one evening while I was working in my home zone. I had just dropped off some reports at the department. And while there, I used the restroom. I then left the station to work some traffic to kill time before going home for my dinner break.

In the space of an hour I made three traffic stops, all of which involved women. After clearing my last stop I headed home for dinner. When I walked into the house, Carole gave me a shocked look and asked what I had been doing. I told her that I had been working traffic, which prompted her to laugh at me. When she finally quieted down, I asked what on earth her laughter was about. As she spoke, she looked down with a smirk on her face.

As I too looked down, I was horrified to discover that not only was my fly open, but my shirttail was hanging four to five inches out of my trousers. What made it even worse was that, after one of my traffic stops, I had left my pocket notebook in my car. Instead of retrieving it, I opted to write down on my trusty palm pilot the information I had obtained from the woman's driver's license, including her height, weight, eye color, hair color, date of birth, and, in addition, her phone numbers. Try explaining that to your wife while you are standing there with your fly open and your shirttail hanging out. Fortunately, Carole already knew that I was an idiot, but it didn't prevent her from making as much fun of me as she could.

* * *

To paraphrase Shakespeare, all is not lost that ends well. It was a Sunday morning. I was on light duty following minor surgery, and I was working the police desk when a gentlemen wearing overalls and resembling Santa Clause approached me with his flowing white hair and beard hanging over his sizable belly.

Let's say that his name was Mr. Borden, who stated that he was wanted in Washington State on the criminal charge of escape, and that he was tired of running.

I patted him down for weapons and invited him to have a seat in the main office while I asked dispatch to run a "wants and warrants" computer search on him.

He looked pretty harmless as he sat there quietly. The dispatcher then called me back to ask if I was "10-12," which was our ten-code to indicate that we needed to get out of earshot of the suspect.

Once I had moved around the desk wall to where I could freely talk, I sarcastically asked the dispatcher, "What's up? Is he an axe murderer or something?"

The dispatcher announced that the man was an escapee from the Washington State Hospital for the criminally insane, where he was serving a life sentence for hacking his parents to pieces.

Needless to say, I couldn't get Mr. Borden into handcuffs fast enough, even if he did look like Santa Claus.

You would think that by then I had learned my lesson, namely, that it is rarely wise to presume an answer to a question you don't know the answer to. And it is even wiser not to blurt out the question when you act like you know the answer for sure.

For some time, I wondered why Santa put lumps of coal into my stocking that Christmas. I guess I was on his naughty list. At least he didn't have to dump the coal on the ground around my tombstone.

Pictured here is retired Sheriff of Missoula County Montana Carl Ibsen. Carl is not only my Brother in Blue, (or Brown in this case) but my Brother in Christ. He has undoubtedly had the greatest impact on my career in addition to being one of my closest friends. But for his and my wife's intervention this story would likely have never been told.

Don & Billie Schultz on their wedding day.

Mark Rosenbaum and I circa 1964 I am on the left

Keith on left, Kenny on Right
The Twins

Law abiding GI. The things you will do on a dare

Graduation From Military Police School This guy surely is too young to be a cop

Carole and I when we first started dating

Wedding Day 1979

Chief G.T. and my graduating members from the Northern Virginia Criminal Justice Academy, March 16, 1982. I'm the handsome devil on the left.

Hey, this kid doesn't even look old enough to be a cop.

Carole, Our first Daughter Kristi and I at my Academy Graduation

Master Police Officer circa 1989.

Casey Gunter and I were hired together

My Father Don Schultz built this for me in 1989 to house items related to my shooting. It may seem a little weird to have the weapon that shot you hanging on your wall, but I know that it is one weapon that will never be used against me or any other Police Officer in the future. Note the hole dead center below the neck line of the vest.

Patrol Car at the crime lab for processing. The orange rod projects the path of the round that struck me in the chest.

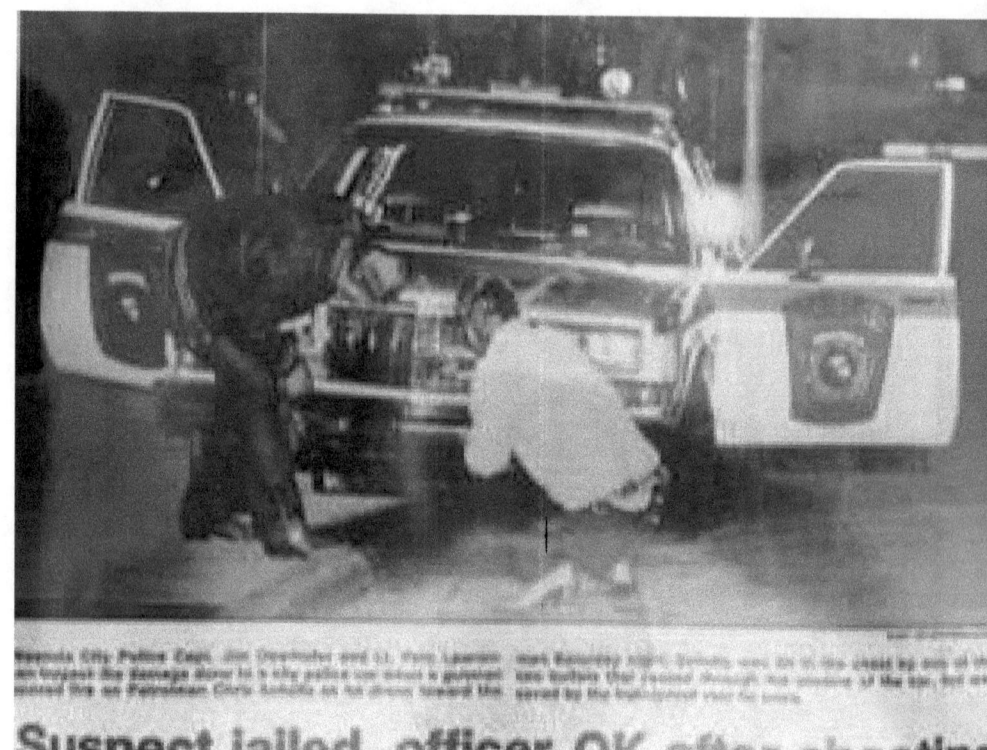

The front-page picture from the Missoulian newspaper Mother's Day morning after the shooting. Detectives are inspecting the bullet hole in the grill. Note the bullet holes in the windshield on both sides of the patrol car.

My son Sam and I at my Graduation from the Highway Patrol Academy in November of 1994

Graduation Picture from the Montana Highway Patrol Academy Badge # 266

The day I was sworn in with the Missoula County Sheriff's Office as Badge # 469. Pictured with me is Sheriff Doug Chase.

The man who gave me the desire to be a Police Officer during my Internship while in High School and the Chief that would hire me at the Missoula City Police Department before his retirement. He would go on to be elected as the Missoula County Sheriff and would hire me there years later.

CHAPTER SEVEN

Every Cop's Worst Nightmare

Most cops believe they are invincible and therefore capable of handling any situation. I was no exception. Whenever my wife worried about me, I teased her, saying, "Hey, I'm Superman. I can handle anything "I often told Carole when she worried about me.

From the very first day, we officers were trained not to become losers. While we didn't wear capes and fly like Superman, we were definitely alpha-type personalities. Up to this point in my career I had never considered the possibility that I might actually be killed on the job. I thought it could happen to someone else, but not to me. I believed that when it was my time to go I could be run over by a truck when crossing the street or die of a sudden heart attack, yet not from taking a bullet.

By now I had been a cop for nine years. Our department did not issue body armor. It was up to the officers to provide their own. I was wearing a second-hand vest I had purchased years before from a fellow Prince William County police officer. The armor was labelled Second Chance brand, level IIA, and contained a front and back panel without side protection. It had begun to wrinkle and get a little stinky-funky in appearance, no matter how often I cleaned it.

As a Christian I still espoused the idea that when it's my time to go, it's my time to go. I could not afford to purchase a new vest, so I considered not wearing the second-hand, tattered one. But as soon as the thought of being without it crossed my mind, the Lord God in his infinite providence impressed upon my heart words that I couldn't ignore: "Hey, you idiot, a carpenter wears a hard hat for the same reason you wear a vest. Leave it on."

Now, I can't say that it was a clear audible voice from God, but it was clear enough to know that I shouldn't argue with it.

* * *

Over the next few weeks I had the feeling that something dreadful was about to happen. But I couldn't quite put my finger on it. I shared my feeling with Carole and we talked and prayed about it.

The, 9th, of May 1987 was a beautiful and unseasonably warm spring evening. I was slated to work the late-night shift. Earlier in the day I had bought Carole a dozen roses for Mother's Day which was the next day. I had purchased flowers for her many times in the past, but this was the first time I had bought a dozen roses. I don't know why I thought to do it, other than to give her a more meaningful and long-overdue token of my love.

As I prepared to leave that night, I had the feeling that whatever had been bothering me was soon to be answered, and I expressed as much to Carole. She asked me to call off working that night. But I told her that I couldn't do so because it would leave us short-shifted. I assured her that all would be fine and I shrugged it off.

Once I arrived for my shift briefing, I was greeted by my sergeant who advised me that a civilian would ride along with me. A Southern Baptist pastor by the name of Bill Moore had recently come to Missoula to start a church, and he had just joined the local ministerial association. At this juncture we had no set departmental chaplain. Ministers from the association would occasionally ride with us and offer their assistance if we ever needed it. Because I was the nominal "Christian" on shift, I was assigned all of the ministers. Regardless of what religion they were, it was assumed that I would be happy to have them accompany me. While I really didn't want any company that night, I agreed as always, and Pastor Moore joined me.

We had barely gotten past our introductions when I fell in behind a vehicle a block from the station. We watched the vehicle cross back and forth over the center and shoulder lines. The driver then turned without stopping for a stop sign. So I conducted a traffic stop and quickly determined that the driver was intoxicated. We returned to the station for processing and then transported the driver to jail.

* * *

A Missoula spring carnival was underway downtown, so I headed towards Front Street where I planned to walk through the carnival. As I turned onto Front Street, I heard the dispatcher send our north, two-officer duty car to where possible shots were being fired at the Super America gas station at the intersection of Front and Orange.

Because the North duty car was on break and I was only a few blocks away, I advised the dispatcher that I would respond. It was then that I made a nearly fatal error of judgement.

During weekends prior to this call, we had experienced a rash of kids shooting paintballs in the downtown area. So I did something no cop should ever do. I assumed that this was just another paintball episode instead of taking it more seriously.

Receiving the dispatcher's call at 11:27 P.M., I drove to where I was advised there was an apparent disturbance between a male and female, which altered my thought process about scouting for paintballs. At 11:28 P.M., I observed a man and a woman in a heated argument at a medical plaza on Front Street, a block and a half west of Orange. The man wore a black leather vest of the kind often worn by local motorcycle gang members. I couldn't see if there were any colors on his vest, but the situation clearly was to be taken more seriously.

The two individuals stood at the entrance to the medical building's horseshoe driveway near the curb on the street's south side. I crossed the street at an angle and stopped at the curb about thirty feet shy of them. The woman's back was turned toward me while the man was partially obscured as he stood facing the woman screaming at her. As I cast my spotlight on them, the man immediately rolled to his left and inserted his hand into his vest. I recognized the motion and realized he was going for a gun in a shoulder holster, like the one I carried when off duty. I was stunned in disbelief.

As he spun around towards me and rushed in my direction with a stainless steel revolver in his hand, and began shooting, I reached for my weapon and the patrol car door as he began to fire. I remember the windshield opening up in front of me as a bullet pierced it. I instantly felt as if someone had kicked me in the chin. Amid the sudden blaze of his muzzle flashes, I had taken a hit to my face.

My first thought was about what would happen to Carole and the kids if I didn't make it. Yet, the inexplicable peace of God came over me, as if to say to me that I need not worry should I live or die, for I was in God's hands and he was in control.

I saw the color red as a rush of adrenalin covered my pain and gave me energy and determination with which to end the attack and put the would-be killer down.

By now the man was lying on my hood and shooting point-blank into the windshield. I immediately recalled from my academy years a similar situation that occurred in another state. A suspect had shot six rounds into a windshield while the officer fired six rounds in return. Both were carrying thirty-eight caliber revolvers but neither was wounded. I was carrying a .357 magnum with ammunition for a .38 Special, which was the limit of firepower the department permitted us to carry.

* * *

We all have experienced the phenomenon of time slowing down, as it did for me for those few split seconds. I had never felt more alive in my entire life nor known such a myriad of thoughts to race through my mind. When I realized that I ought not shoot through the windshield, I also realized that to exit the car would be to abandon what little cover I had. And I didn't want Pastor Bill to be left there exposed, should I be killed.

A month earlier, I had attended an officer survival seminar put on by Ron McCarthy and Associates. I remembered being taught to back out of the kill zone during an ambush. So I laid down in the seat and tried to find reverse gear, but I missed it. I then recalled the instructor saying that, if plans A, and B don't work out, don't just sit there but make something up.

It occurred to me that I was driving a three-thousand pound weapon. So I jammed the vehicle into drive and crushed the accelerator to the floor. The suspect's knees were against my bumper as he lay on the hood, shooting his gun. As the car accelerated, he flew over top of the driver's-side spotlight as I looked directly into his eyes. I knew I was staring death in the face, for he was hell-bent upon killing me.

After upending him with the car, I also struck the woman before demolishing a parking meter on the curb, scattering loose change all over the street. I angled the car to the opposite side and came to rest on the far curb. I remember glancing at Pastor Bill and telling him to stay in the car as I exited my door and ran for cover to the doorway of another medical building.

Once behind cover I notified dispatch that I had been shot and requested backup. But I couldn't understand why I received no response. I later learned that I had experienced what is referred to as auditory exclusion, an anomaly that affects some people under stress, temporarily shutting down their hearing.

In retrospect, I had called for backup at 11:29 P.M., which was only two minutes from the moment I had received dispatch's instruction to travel to where I suddenly found myself in the middle of a one-sided gun fight that lasted for all of thirty to forty-seconds. But it seemed like an eternity.

While I ran for cover, the suspect got back up on his feet and pointed his revolver at me. I could not return fire since he was standing behind the woman with her back facing me. I could see nothing of him except part of his face and his hand holding the gun over her shoulder. The desire to shoot back was never stronger, but I resisted the urge lest I strike the woman who posed no immediate threat to me.

From the cover of the building's doorway, I ordered the suspect to drop his weapon. I must have screamed quite loudly because the next morning my voice was gone. After what seemed like hours but was only minutes, the suspect dropped his gun to the pavement and lay prone as I had ordered.

Looking back on that moment, I don't believe he actually responded to my command. I believe he responded to the eight additional officers who had arrived on the scene in response to my call for assistance. Due to my momentary tunnel vision and auditory exclusion, I had not been aware of their presence.

As the suspect lay on the ground, I crossed back into the street toward him to take him into custody, at which point the woman began to advance toward me. She was angry and distraught, screaming at me as I demanded that she stop and lie down. But she did not heed my requests.

I felt myself getting light-headed and my legs going wobbly. I did not see a weapon in her hand, but I noted a sheathed knife on her belt. Flashing through my mind was the statistic that twenty-five percent of officers who die, do so by their own or their partner's handgun. I determined then and there that I was not going to be a willing victim.

The woman was about ten feet from me and still advancing when I drew a bead on her chest and began to pull the trigger. I vividly recall seeing the hammer pull back on my service revolver as I determined that I would shoot before letting her get on top of me, for I was all but moments from collapse.

Thankfully, it was a shot I did not need to take. At that very moment I heard Officer Greg Willoughby step up beside me and say, "Chris, I've got her." His were the first words I had heard throughout the entire encounter.

I then became aware of other officers closing in on us from all sides. I can't explain why my hearing returned at that exact moment, but I don't think it was an accident. Ironically, Greg, also a Christian, stepped up as I was about to shoot to take the woman's life. To this very day, I still thank God for Greg and his timing.

After Greg took over, I stumbled to the curb and sat down. As I then reached up to feel my face and chin, I realized I did not have a serious wound. As I gazed at Officers Rich Oschner and Jim Neumayer coming to my aid, I swore, "I couldn't believe that (expletive) shot me." Even now, I regret letting those words slip from my mouth. Others later said to me that it was the first time they thought of me as human, for they had never heard me curse before.

* * *

Rich and Jim laid me down and stripped off my shirt and vest. I was puzzled as to why they had removed my vest until they told me that I had been shot in the chest. At first, I was jubilant at the thought that the vest had apparently done what it should, but then I feared that it hadn't stopped the bullet.

The vest indeed had done its job. I was not in pain at the time because adrenalin was still coursing through my veins. Soon, however, I felt like I had been run over by a truck. As I looked around, I was so thankful to my fellow officers for the way in which they were caring for me and tending to the crime scene. They had done a fantastic job.

While awaiting an ambulance, I heard a radio transmission that horrified me. Although he was not yet on the scene, and having no idea as to my condition, the shift captain had advised dispatch to call my wife and tell her that I had been shot. His request was strictly against departmental policy. I remember grabbing Jim Neumayer's arm and saying, "Please don't let them make that call."

Jim was distraught as well. But he could not countermand his captain. Despite the captain's mistake, I bore him no ill will. His brother had been killed in the line of duty a few years before I was hired, and I couldn't begin to imagine what was going through his mind at the moment.

If ever I were to hand-pick an officer to inform my family that I had been injured or killed on the job, it would be Officer Tom Johnson. Tom was a friend and one of the most compassionate officers I had ever met. He was gentle and kind and a very capable policeman. Tom was working the South side of Missoula that night and realized as he listened to the radio traffic that he could not quickly get to me from where he was. Yet he instinctively knew that someone needed to go to Carole to be with her. So when he heard the captain give the dispatcher the order to call Carole, he was already on his way to my house and stepped up his response, literally sliding into my driveway in order to beat the phone call from dispatch.

When Carole answered the door, Tom asked if she had gotten a phone call. She said she had not. He then told Carole that I had been shot, but also that he had heard me on the radio and thought I might be okay. Carole could not comprehend how anyone could be shot and still be okay. Tom reminded her that I always wore my vest and that he would take her to the hospital to see me. She was walking out the door in a daze when Tom asked about the kids who were asleep. Carole was too much in shock and began to cry, not knowing what to do. Our neighbor across the street, Suzanne Davies, had heard Tom pull up moments before. She realized that something must be wrong for Tom to respond as he had. Suzanne gratefully offered to stay with the kids until Carole returned.

* * *

Although we did not discover it until a day or so later, another miracle had occurred that night. The dispatcher had been unable to reach Carole on the phone because of having called the wrong number.

Just that week, as it turned out, the 911 center had redone our response code sheet, which was used by all officers in the area to keep track of the ten-codes and report disposition codes. The code sheet also contained the phone number of every law enforcement officer in Missoula County.

If my memory serves me correctly, there were about 120 numbers on the list. Whoever had compiled the numbers had transposed two digits of my phone number. Mine was the only wrong number on the list.

By then a pattern was developing. The odds were astronomical that so many fortunate things had happened to me that same night. And they didn't stop there. Not being a believer in mere coincidences, I am a believer in providential occurrences.

About the time that Tom arrived at my front door to inform Carole, the ambulance had transported me to St. Patrick's Hospital a block away from the scene.

In just about every city and town in this country, cops and medical professionals in emergency rooms are more than just casual acquaintances to police officers. This is true for two reasons. First, we police officers spend a lot of time in emergency rooms with victims and suspects alike. So we get to know the medical professionals. Second, we cops realize that if something really terrible ever happens to us, our friends in the medical profession will pull out all the stops to save us.

My nurse that night was Deb Corrigan. She was married to one of my partners, Tom Corrigan, who worked in the Missoula County jail. Deb was holding things together pretty well until she saw Carole come in with Tom Johnson.

Carole was almost five months pregnant at the time, with what would have been our fifth child. When Deb saw Carole, she began to tear up as she sensed the impact of what could have happened had I not been wearing my armor. Doctor Webber, the emergency room physician on duty, checked me out and removed shrapnel from the surface of my face, chin, and left arm, which instinctively I had held up to protect my face when the suspect started shooting. After x-rays and treatment for superficial wounds, he released me.

While I was still being treated, Detective Tom Wivel interviewed Pastor Bill Moore who, having been checked out by the emergency personnel, was found to be uninjured. Tom asked Bill what had happened. Bill stated that everything occurred just as I had reported it. He mentioned my receiving the dispatcher's call and then pulling up at an angle to the curb, shining my spotlight on the suspect. He continued to say how the suspect rolled out from the spotlight, pulled out the gun from inside his vest, and fired upon us as he rushed my car.

Bill confirmed that the suspect fired a total of five shots and that two of them were aimed at his side of the car, with the other three directed at me. He said that he had heard all but the second shot.

To have said that Detective Wivel was incredulous at Pastor Bill's recollection would have been an understatement. Most the time it is difficult enough getting witnesses even to talk about what they have seen, much less in so much detail.

Detective Wivel asked Bill why he didn't hear the second round shot, and Bill said, "At that point God was telling me to sit back and enjoy the ride because everything was going to be okay."

Wivel later told me that he had asked Moore to repeat the story again, because he had pretty much decided that Moore could not possibly have had such accurate recall. But his doubt turned to respect and amazement when the crime lab's ballistics conducted its investigation and found everything to scientifically corroborated exactly as Bill had stated.

Presumably, the first round of bullets had hit the grill and radiator of my patrol car. The second round had hit just left of the hood ornament. Two of the remaining rounds struck the windshield on my side of the car, the first hitting the windshield wiper, separating it into pieces of shrapnel that struck my face and arm. The following round hit slightly higher and passed through the windshield and under the steering wheel, striking me dead-center between the top two buttons of my uniform shirt. The bullet came to rest in the front plate pocket of my vest.

I was later told, by one of the investigators of Al Kimery's shooting, that I was hit in almost the same spot on my shirt as Al was.

The last round struck Bill's seat where his shoulder would normally have been. It hit precisely where the vinyl at the edge of the seat met the fabric. Bill didn't remember moving, but he believed that God had moved him out of the way of the bullet. After all of the timely good fortune that had occurred up to that point, who was I to argue that it was not God at work?

As a side note, everyone else in the ministerial association disappeared from volunteering after that night. Bill, however, returned the next weekend to everyone's amazement, and went on to become our first regular departmental chaplain. His courage garnered great respect among my fellow officers, because so many had thought they would never see him again.

* * *

After Dr. Weber released me to go home, I opted instead to go to the station to write my report while it was fresh on my mind. My lieutenant, Gary Lancaster, and his wife Gail had come to the hospital to check on me. Gary was off duty when the shooting occurred but was notified since one of his officers was involved. Gary and Gail drove Carole and me to the station.

An additional bright spot at this point in the evening was knowing that the patrol car I was to drive was not my regular one, and therefore not subject to processing. But those hopes were dashed when I passed it on a wrecker on the way to the station. For it had been involved in an accident during a pursuit about an hour after my shooting. Oh well, I thought, that was minor compared to what I had just lived through.

I had recently purchased the uniform shirt I was wearing at the time of the shooting, which had been seized as evidence. I figured that it too was a loss. After all, it was my life that had been spared and I shouldn't complain. Patrol cars and uniform shirts could easily be replaced, but I could not. To this day, that shirt, that vest, and the revolver that shot me, all hang in a case in my man cave as a reminder that each new day of life is a gift.

Upon arriving at the station, I started what I thought would become the masterpiece report of my career. I was usually a great report writer. But it was not possible for me to know just how much the incident had affected me. When reading it later, I realized that it had been a mistake to do the report that night. It was a mess, to say the least. A rookie fresh out of the academy could have done better. Thank God that the other officers did superb work with theirs that night. It's highly unusual for people to volunteer to be witnesses to what they have seen. But that night I received one of the best compliments ever given an officer, which was the support of the community. I really didn't need to write a report, because every conceivable angle was covered by witnesses who had watched the events unfold. Even the chief public defender was a witness for me.

That night and in the days to follow, Carole and I enjoyed many well wishes from fellow officers. They will never know how much that meant to us. We did not leave the station until a little before seven o'clock on the morning of May 10, 1987. When we got home, neither Carole nor I could sleep. The night had been a harrowing one, and we had not decompressed. While talking and comparing notes, one of the greatest miracles came to light.

Carole always read her Bible every night before kneeling next to the bed to pray for me. The night of the shooting was no exception. She had just completed praying when she heard the sirens. She knew something big must be happening, so she made a mental note of the time on the clock that sat next to our bed. That time was 11:28 P.M.

We both later agreed that she had been praying for me at the exact moment I was attacked. As I said before, I am not a believer in coincidences. It is my belief that the power of God was at work. Life in all of its astonishing mystery simply cannot be predicated upon a rash of mere coincidences.

Consider the fact that the suspect was identified as Clark Theodore Johnson, whom the weekend before I had encountered on the street over an open container of beer, in front of a local biker bar just a few short blocks from where he shot me a week later. Missoula had an ordinance prohibiting open containers on the street. Since we were busy at the time, I ushered him back into the bar instead of writing him a ticket for the violation. While he was cooperative, I could tell by the expression on his face that he had no use for police. But I didn't realize at the time just how much he actually disliked us.

On three occasions over the period of many years, Johnson had threatened police and his own family members with his firearms. While he never made a definitive statement admitting his guilt, he maintained that he shot at me because I was trying to run him down. His claim was clearly debunked by all of the witnesses who stated that I had not run at him until he had already fired upon me. He did say that he thought there were two officers in the car and that he was shooting at both of them. Had Pastor Moore not been with me, then all five rounds would have been aimed at my side of the car. The result could possibly have proven fatal. So, was it strictly coincidental or by mere chance that I was not killed? I don't believe so. I believe it was providential.

On the night of the shooting, I concluded that Clark Johnson was shooting at a blue uniform that just happened to show up in the wrong place at the wrong time, or perhaps the right place at the right time, depending upon one's perspective.

Shortly after the shooting, Officers Rich Oschner and Rick Dahlgren, who had been riding in the North duty car that night, approached me to thank me. They were the ones for whom I had taken the call. They told me their lives were probably saved because, had they answered the call themselves, they most likely would have pulled right up to the suspects and through the patrol car window asked them what was going on. Had they done so, they would have had little to no time to react to Johnson as he reached for his gun to shoot.

Was it by sheer coincidence that I had taken the call for Officers Oschner and Dahlgren? I don't believe so.

* * *

The next morning, Carole and I spoke to our children and told them what had happened. Even though they were young, we knew that their peers would be curious. Then, too, the media would likely be at our doorstep.

It had been three years since Missoula had lost Al Kimery. The fact that my body armor had saved my life was big news. Kristi was six at the time and Kimberly four. Kristi had a better grasp of what was going on, while Kimberly less so. A few days prior to the shooting, Kimberly had worn through the toes of a pair of shoes designated for church, after being told not to ride a certain toy in my parents driveway with those shoes on her feet. As a result she got a spanking.

Knowing that I had been shot, Kim then wanted to know whether I would be spanked for getting holes in my shirt. And I had to admit that she had a point.

That morning was Mother's Day, with special activities planned at the church, so we decided to go since we couldn't sleep. But it turned out to be a mistake since most people are not familiar with the stress that such a traumatic incident creates.

My pastor at the time asked me to give a public testimony as to how God had spared my life the night before. He meant well, and I didn't blame him for wanting to bless the congregation, but I was neither prepared nor eager to do that. The experience was still fresh. I could not get the face of Clark Johnson out of my mind. So I gave a very brief synopsis of what was contained in the department's press release. It was good to receive the congregational members' love for us after the services, but both Carole's and my nerves were beyond being frayed. We went home that afternoon and slept while my parents took care of the kids.

I spent the following week trying to decompress and comprehend what had happened. I agreed to speak with a local newspaper reporter who came to our house for an interview. I was not prepared, however, to see my face plastered in an 8x10 glossy in the next day's edition of the paper. As a consequence of the photo, people recognized me on the street, which for a cop was a bit unnerving even though they certainly meant well.

I went into a local pet store one afternoon to exchange some fish for our fish tank. A lady recognized me and thanked me for my service to the community, and then she promptly asked to buy the fish that I had just returned to the store owner. Missoula doesn't get many celebrities, so I guess it was my turn to be in the fish bowl, vicariously speaking. Carole and I had a good laugh about the incident when I got home.

The scripture says, "A merry heart doeth good like a medicine: but a broken spirit drieth the bones" (Prov 17:22). The Lord knew that we needed a good laugh right about then. It isn't always the big miracles that are important. Sometimes the little ones lighten the spirit.

The following Friday was Kristi's graduation from Kindergarten, which was yet another public appearance for me that I really wasn't ready to make. But what could I do? I had given a child safety talk to Kristi's class a few weeks before. So, on the occasion of Kristi's commencement, a little boy from the class ran up to me and asked, "Officer Schultz, were you the officer that was shot?"

I told him that I was. He then asked, "Did you shoot the bad guy?"

"No," I replied, "I ran over him with my car."

The youngster turned and ran with a horrified look on his face, exclaiming, "You're mean!"

I suppose I would have been just fine in his eyes had I shot Clark Johnson. While the boy's remark was humorous, I must admit that I feared how children and even some of my own family would look upon me differently because of what I had been through.

* * *

For the first week after the shooting, I reflected on how I had reacted. And I came to the conclusion that there was nothing I could have done differently, except perhaps to take the dispatcher's call more seriously at the beginning.

My thinking remained abstract. But that soon changed drastically.

The night after Kristi's kindergarten graduation, I rushed Carole to the hospital. She suffered from a condition called toxemia, a medical term for out-of-control blood pressure during pregnancy. The physician discovered it during her pregnancy with Kimberly. We had already lost Benjamin, and nearly lost Melissa in the delivery room due to placental problems spurred on by the toxemia. The week had taken its toll on both of us physically and mentally. The end result was that Carole lost our baby. The stress was simply too much for her and for me.

I tried earnestly to make sense of it and to come to terms with why this had happened. But I could only blame Clark Johnson for our loss. Thus began my two-year odyssey into bitterness, which nearly destroyed me and my family. God doesn't promise us that life will be fair, nor does he promise that life will always be good. But he does promise that he will never saddle us with more than we can handle. "There hath no temptation taken you but such as is common to man: but God is faithful, who will not suffer you to be tempted above that ye are able; but will with the temptation also make a way to escape, that ye may be able to bear it" (I Cor 10:13).

God also promises that wherever we go he will be with us. So it is incumbent upon us to keep our eyes on him. During my lifetime I have discovered that every time I reached a peak, Satan sought to throw a curve ball in an effort to trip me up and destroy me. For the last thing that Satan wants is for God to receive the glory that Satan covets for himself.

For the next two years following the shooting in which I was nearly killed, I allowed Satan to take me to the woodshed by taking my eyes off of the Lord. Yes, I allowed this to happen in spite of God's greatest saving moment in my life. I took my eyes off of the Master and paid the price, not because God made it so, but because he afforded me the same free will that he bestows upon all of us.

For reasons that I now explain, I allowed myself to be consumed by bitterness. I permitted myself to play right into Satan's hand. I grieved God deeply during those two years, but I am thankful that he is a forgiving God who wrapped his arms around me after my season of bitterness.

Before I could return to work, the police department required that I see a psychologist at the University of Montana, a gentleman who happened to have absolutely no background in law enforcement. While he was nice enough, I basically wrote him off when I discovered that he had no real knowledge of my job. I answered his questions and told him what he wanted to hear so that I could "get back on the horse," so to speak.

I later learned that this was one of the most common responses that cops have after a critical incident. I also later learned that the instant desire to return to work is a warning sign to police psychologists who deal with these situations on a regular basis. Unfortunately, my department had not fully come to understand such matters, which was a common phenomenon among smaller jurisdictions during those days.

I returned to work, but things got rapidly worse. For one, I was exceedingly claustrophobic when getting into a patrol car. Then, at night I experienced nightmares about the shooting, and flashbacks during the day. Yet I was determined to get back in the saddle even though Carole knew that I wasn't ready for it. More importantly, deep down within my own heart I knew I wasn't ready for it either.

I was afraid to express my unreadiness because of the stigma attached to my actual condition, which I eventually learned to be post-traumatic stress disorder.

Looking back, and knowing what I now know, I firmly believe that many of my problems could have been eliminated, or at least mitigated, had the department conducted a debriefing with me after the incident. Had someone come to me and said, "Chris, it is normal to be claustrophobic after going through a critical incident in a confined space like a patrol car." Or, "Chris, it's natural to have nightmares after a critical incident. Not only is it natural, but in time the nightmares will diminish."

Certainly, the department should have done this, but it didn't, and not due to any malice on its part, but simply because the department had not taken the time to become informed and receive the necessary training. What is nearly universal standard practice today was not the case then.

* * *

An unexpected development arose with regard to some of my fellow officers. Most of them were quite understanding and appreciative of the fact that I was still in the department. Yet some of them were not so supportive. Several criticized me, especially older ones who thought that I should have shot Clark Johnson. Some went so far as to say that I was egregiously wrong for not doing so.

I had come to doubt all that I had believed about how well I had responded to the situation that night. And not only because of critical comments from fellow officers, but because of the anger and bitterness that I continued to harbor toward Clark Johnson for being responsible, if only indirectly, for the death of our child.

Criticisms even came from other departments as the story spread throughout the Missoula law enforcement community.

Yet, most of the critics, once they heard from me the story in its entirety, came to understand that they probably would have reacted in the same way. At the same time, those who had already made up their minds continued to spread a false narrative, one that still prevailed eight years later, as I discovered when speaking with a city officer who later became the chief of the Missoula Police Department.

By that time, while working for the Montana Highway Patrol, I had met a city officer one quiet night in a local parking lot and congratulated him on his recent promotion to sergeant. As we were talking, he brought up the matter of my shooting. I asked him what he had heard. He candidly stated that the word was that I had screwed up that night. And I was shocked.

So I asked him if he wanted to hear the real story. At the conclusion he agreed, as did so many others, that I had done all I should have done. He also shared that some officers had said that I had not approached the scene safely, and, just as some in my own department had said, that I should have shot the suspect.

Invariably, those reports were from officers who were not on duty the night of my shooting. It is so easy to be a Monday morning quarterback when you have not been in the game. Even so, I had largely, though not largely enough, laid that matter to rest some years earlier.

Law enforcement is a brotherhood and sisterhood, I said to myself. But people still are human, and cops gossip just like everyone else.

* * *

For the next two years things got only worse for me. I arrived one day a few months after the shooting at the Missoula County Jail with a prisoner I had arrested. It had been but a few months since the shooting. I was in the process of unholstering my pistol in order to place it in a lock box before entering the jail.

As I stepped off of the elevator, I was stunned to see Clark Johnson sweeping the floor in the foyer of the gun locker room.

Rage welled up within of me. For here stood a man who twice had been charged with deliberately attempted homicide. To my dumbfounded eyes Johnson had become a trustee in the jail system, a trustee being a prisoner given extra privileges usually involving basic maintenance tasks in the facility.

A police officer had been the target of one of those homicides. Moreover, three prior incidents involved Johnson who had been a police officer himself years before. He had pulled a weapon on an officer who had responded to a domestic disturbance at Johnson's home. Subsequently, Johnson worked as a dispatcher in the same region, repeating the same offense for the same reason once again, although against a different officer who likewise had responded to a domestic disturbance at Johnson's home.

In the late 1970s or early 1980s, Johnson had been arrested in Missoula after a SWAT team was summoned to his residence where he had barricaded himself and his family during yet one more domestic dispute.

Johnson was familiar with police tactics. So, there he stood in front of me, precisely where officers routinely removed their weapons to place them in gun lockers, though he didn't appear to recognize me as I walked past him.

After turning over my prisoner, I asked to speak with the shift supervisor. It was he from whom I learned that Johnson had become a so-called "trustee" because—get this—he baked good cookies.

I then contacted my shift sergeant, Steve Ross, who was as astonished as I was. He went up the chain of command in the police department, which then went up the chain of command of the sheriff's department, and within an hour I received notification that the situation had been rectified. Johnson was back in his cell where he belonged.

The incident served only to increase my depression. It left me with a sense of abandonment by more fellow officers. The suspect in Al Kimery's death received no such special privilege as Johnson.

I concluded that the general consensus in much of the local law enforcement community at the time was: "Your vest saved you. So what's the big deal?"

The big deal for me was that, except for the remnant of some cloth fabric and a ballistic plate, I would have left behind a widow and three children without their father, plus three brothers, a sister, and a mother and father. While my physical wounds from Johnson's .357 magnum had long since healed, except for the indentation in my sternum which took years to disappear, the psychological wounds remained open and festering.

When I began my career, I was prepared to take another's life if it ever became necessary. But the circumstances of that fateful night left me with the feeling that somehow I had failed for not having discharged my weapon. I now know that, had I taken Johnson's life and possibly his wife's, I would have carried yet another heavy burden of guilt no matter how justified I may have been in doing so.

Even today, I hope I will never again be in that position. The primary difference is that now the resources exist for assisting officers through the maze of emotions that accompany the misery of post-traumatic stress disorder.

***

When Clark Johnson's trial came about, I believed I would gain a sense of closure and the nightmares and related issues would go away. As a way of coping, I poured myself into my job until the trial. I worked every overtime detail I could under the guise of taking care of my family. In reality, I was using overtime as an excuse to stay busy. I reasoned that a lack of sleep would eliminate my nightmares. But working long hours and depriving myself of deep rest only compounded the problem in that I grew temperamentally short with my family, which unfortunately became the norm.

On the day the trial was set to start, I was more than ready to see justice served to Clark Johnson. Instead, he offered an Alford plea to avoid a trial that he knew he would lose. An Alford plea basically states that when there is enough evidence to convict a defendant, the defendant refuses to plead guilty. In my conflicted state of mind, this seemed to be yet another instance of dashed hopes for the vindication of my actions. The only real consolation I received during Johnson's sentencing was to hear the judge state that if he could have legally charged Johnson for the death of our unborn child, he would have done so. Unfortunately, Montana law did not permit it.

The only plausible explanation that Adult Probation and Parole could come up with, as an explanation of Johnson's actions at the time of the shooting, was that he had been riding with the local Bandito motorcyclist chapter. And, while he was not yet a chapter prospect, he would have achieved instant recognition had he successfully killed me and gotten away with it. Adult Probation and Parole did not believe that he was specifically out on the street that night to kill a police officer, but rather that I was a target of opportunity when I arrived upon the scene.

The prearranged sentence dealt me still another insult. Johnson received two sixty-year sentences for attempting to kill Bill Moore and me. The sentences were to run concurrently, not consecutively, meaning that Johnson could be out of prison in fourteen and a half years if he behaved. To me that seemed like a paltry price to pay for the death of my child and my own near death, as well as for the stress I was enduring. A promising outcome quickly turned into what I considered to be the defeat of any personal vindication I might have received for all of the turmoil that my family and I had endured.

From the sentencing on, I became more and more depressed. The only place I seemed to function well was at work. I made a lot of arrests, answered many calls, was quick to back up my peers, and worked a ton of street traffic. I had one of the top arrest and citations records in the department that year. When the time arrived for the Missoula Policeman's Ball, the patrol captain pulled me into his office. The ball was the occasion for singling out officers in recognition of their service to the department. The captain informed me that I had initially been picked to receive the officer of the year award, but that they then decided not give it to me, lest people think I was awarded it merely because I had been shot.

As I left the event, I thought to myself, what point was there to telling me this? I could have cared less about the award. But being informed in this manner left me feeling that I had been kicked in the groin and spat upon for all of my efforts throughout the year. While the episode was extremely hurtful at the time, I have long ago made peace with it. I mention it now, not to garner sympathy, but in the hope that some present or future police administrator will avoid the mistake of making such an insensitive statement to an officer who deserves recognition.

As I continued throwing myself into my work to ease my pain, I became all the more distant from my family. I loved them with all of my heart, yet I had a hard time dealing with the noise and chaos surrounding the children. They were good kids just being kids. It got to a point that they never came to me for anything. They knew "no" was the answer I would give them. So, what was the point of their asking? I regret those days and have spent years since trying to make it up to them. Unfortunately, some things can't be replicated, such as the children's activities I missed while working to soothe my own needs and selfishness. Bitterness has a tendency to consume the one who is bitter, slowly and surely destroying him. It is as Saint Peter said to Simon the sorcerer, "For I perceive that thou art in the gall of bitterness" (Acts 8:23a), which is not a healthy state to be in before God or man.

* * *

Everything started coming to a head on May 1, 1989, just six days shy of the second anniversary of my shooting. I was working evening shift and noticed a vehicle driving somewhat erratically. I pulled in behind it and turned on my overheads in an effort to stop the driver. The car did not stop but slowed down. I thought this odd and requested another unit to head my way. The vehicle then turned off of the main road and into a vacant lot behind some businesses, proceeding all the way into the darkest portion of the lot, and there it stopped.

The hair stood up on the back of my neck, indicating my hyper-vigilance. And I discovered that my experience of tunnel vision during the first critical incident did not repeat itself then or thereafter. If anything, my awareness became more acute! My backup was still moments away, so I focused all of my spotlights on the suspect's vehicle and quietly opened my door.

As I stepped out of my car, I drew my weapon and held it at my side. My intention was to wait for backup. But as I stepped out of my seat, the driver's door of the suspect's car popped open and I saw that his hand was holding a long-barreled revolver. As he sought to exit his car, the gun's barrel hooked on the inside door handle, causing the suspect to lose his grip of it as it fell to the ground.

By this time I was aiming my own pistol at him. For I had made the decision that I was not going to be shot again. I ordered him not to reach for his gun; and that if he did, I said would shoot him.

He ceased reaching for it even as his hand hovered over it for a second. He must have thought better of going for it, because he stood up. When my backup officer arrived, we took the man into custody. Oddly enough, just as was the case with Clark Johnson, the gun he possessed was a Ruger .357 Magnum.

While I had handled the stop and the arrest quite well, the incident was the beginning of a seemingly uncontrollable downward spiral that could end in only but one of two ways, either with my remaining in a state of irrepressible bitterness or with my gaining victory over it. So, the question posed itself to me. Was I boxed in?

After the incident, my nightmares returned with a vengeance. I began to think that I had lost my mind. I desperately wanted to get back to the person I was before my shooting. I was afraid to ask for help because I feared that my peers would believe I was weak.

I continued to sign up for as much overtime as possible, but this no longer sufficed. As my depression worsened, so did my thoughts of suicide, which I quickly rejected when thinking I could not do that to Carole and the four children we had by then. I was so miserable by this point that you could hardly have beat me to a gun call when one went out over the radio. It wasn't that I craved the action, it was that I hoped someone would end my misery and thus allow Carole and the kids to live off of my death benefits.

Simply to write these words impresses me with just how desperately self-absorbed I had become. No self-worthy esteem remained. I selfishly simply wanted to end it all.

* * *

By now Carole was fed up. Yet she continued to love me in spite of myself, wanting to help me through the darkness into the light. So, being at the end of her rope, she reached out to the one person she believed could help me turn things around—Carl Ibsen.

She asked Carl to come over one evening while I was at work. She laid out all that had happened and requested Carl's insight and assistance. He was by no means blind to what was going on. He had noticed changes in me and realized that they were not for the good.

When I arrived home after work that night, I was surprised to see Carl and Carole sitting in my living room, waiting for me. When I sat down, they gave me an ultimatum: Seek help myself, or they would force me to seek help. Although I wasn't pleased with being bushwhacked, I admitted that I could no longer carry on like nothing was wrong.

Carl asked me to contact my shift sergeant to let him know what was going on. During my next work day my sergeant Steve Ross accompanied me to the chief's office so that I could inform him of what was going on. The meeting did not go well. By then we had a new chief who thought that the matter had already been sufficiently handled right after the shooting. But he had not taken the time to actually study the nature of PTSD. If he had, he would have discovered that I manifested the same behaviors as most cops who struggled with PTSD in that era.

At one point in the conversation, Carole spoke up to interject what she and our kids had lived through the previous two years. The chief angrily told her that she was not his employee nor was she his concern. Had it not been for Sergeant Ross standing over my shoulder, pressing me down, I probably would have done something regrettable.

In the end, the chief agreed to get me help. He decided that I would move to the department's front desk for a light-duty assignment while I was in treatment. Nothing was to be said to other officers, yet within a day or so it was obvious that someone had dropped the information, because the details of my situation had spread throughout the department like wildfire. Many a negative comment was spoken and heard behind my back, and some to my face, about the fact that I was going nuts.

From the front desk I eventually moved to the detective division where I spent the next few months.

* * *

The only police department sufficiently close to Missoula, with a PTSD focus group for officers, was in Spokane, Washington. But the chief decided that the two hundred mile trip was too far and the cost too expensive to send me. So I was referred to a new psychologist who was assisting the department.

The psychologist was helpful to me, but I received more help from meeting with a PTSD group at the local Veterans Affairs center. Even though the experiences of combat vets were different, they were similar enough to mine that I began to understand the disorder. For the first time I understood that I wasn't going crazy, and that the issues I'd been having were natural for someone who'd suffered as I had. And so I began to make peace with it.

One of the key turning points came when the counselor leading the sessions pointed out to me that while I had been trying to regain a sense of normalcy over the past two years, what I failed to recognize was that I needed to embrace the new normal that street combat had fostered.

* * *

During this same period of time a series of meetings took place at our church. One of the pastors who came to speak with us was from Red Deer, Alberta, Canada. I had never met him before, but throughout the day I felt the Lord urging me to speak with him. By the end of the evening, I could no longer put off the encounter. His name was Chuck Colson.

I walked up and introduced myself, saying that I sensed the Lord nudging me to speak to him. I told him that frankly I wasn't sure why. He asked me if something was troubling me. I explained the PTSD issues I was having as a result of the shooting. He smiled and exclaimed that he knew exactly why the Lord had sent me to him.

Pryor to becoming a pastor, Chuck Colson had been an Ontario Provincial policeman in Canada and had suffered from a situation similar to mine. Because of it, he too had struggled with PTSD. We spoke at length, and again during the week's meetings.

Pastor Colson helped me to understand that the root cause of my issue was not the shooting, but rather the bitterness I held towards my assailant and, by then, also the department.

At first, I thought this was crazy. How could anyone expect me to forgive a man who had intentionally tried to murder me, and indirectly murdered our unborn child? And how could I forgive a police department that I believed had hung me out to dry?

Like peeling an onion, Pastor Colson took me through scripture passages that offered me exactly what I needed to do. He helped me understand that bitterness is like a self-destroying cancer, and that by its very nature it sought to envelop me and those around me through my own words and actions. Bitterness, coupled to an unforgiving heart, was the sin of which I was guilty. Clark Johnson wasn't the one destroying me and my family. I was!

If Christ forgave my sins, then how could I deny the same forgiveness to one who had sinned against me? "For the heaven is high above the earth, so great is his mercy toward them that fear him. As far was the East is from the West, so far hath he removed our transgressions from us" (Ps 103:11, 12:11).

Pastor Colson also told me that going back to the scene and reliving the event would be therapeutic. He suggested that I pray over each action that I had taken that evening, asking the Lord to show me how I might have done differently. I had been avoiding the location like a plague, but I did what he asked. I relived the incident and prayed as he advised me. I also studied the passages of scripture he gave me. The scripture that helped me the most was from Ephesians. "Let all bitterness, and wrath and anger, and clamour, and evil speaking, be put away from you, with all malice. And be ye kind one to another, tenderhearted, forgiving one another as God for Christ's sake hath forgiven you" (Eph 4:31).

On the day that I relived the scene and prayed, the burden of guilt and bitterness I had carried for more than two years lifted from my shoulders. I can't say that my nightmares stopped completely. Even today, I still feel somewhat claustrophobic in confined spaces or crowds, but I have learned to acknowledge and work with the smothering feeling.

As for Clark Johnson, I considered how it would be best to contact him. I thought of going to the Montana State Prison to speak with him. But I decided that this was not my best option for reasons of safety. He was not the only criminal I had sent to the prison. A day or so later, when driving past one of our supermarkets, I spotted in its parking lot a vehicle attached to a trailer with the Rock of Ages Prison Ministry logo on it. Seeing a gentleman climbing into the vehicle, I pulled in.

We spoke for some time. I asked where he was headed. He said he was going to the Montana State Prison to hold some meetings. I asked him if he would be willing to track down Clark Johnson and give him a message from me. He agreed to do so. So I wrote a letter to Johnson, stating that I forgave him for what he had done to me, and also that I believed he owed a debt to society, for which purpose he was where he needed to be. I enclosed a gospel tract and told him that I bore no ill will against him, and that I would pray for him to open his life to Christ. I left the department's address for him to contact me if he wished. The minister was glad to receive the letter and to pass it on.

I never heard from Johnson, but I so much wish that I had. I can honestly say that if I were to meet him today on the street, I would shake his hand and wish him well. I don't believe a "bromance" would come of it, but I do believe it is the right way to lay down such a burden. Little did Clark Johnson know that his attempt to take Pastor Moore's and my life would change the whole direction of my life and my family's life. What was meant for evil came back tenfold for good: It is difficult to say thank you for something that brought us so much pain, but apart from those restorative efforts we would not be the close family that we are today. Nor would we have the extended family that we now have with our sons-in-law and daughters-in-law. God has been truly good to us.

***

As for the Missoula Police Department, the actions of a few had stirred my nest to make it uncomfortable for me to stay. Had things not been as they were, I would never have had the desire to leave. And yet, the same forgiveness that I had extended to Clark Johnson I owed to the department. Over the coming months I made peace with every officer in the department. This set the stage for the next chapter of my life.

My shooting had impacted the department in positive as well as negative ways. For one thing, it now had a permanent police chaplain in Bill Moore whose personal witness led the captain and the lieutenant of detectives to Christ, along with other officers. In addition, the department came to realize the importance of body armor. And not only the department, but also the Missoula County Sheriff's Department began issuing armor to its deputies.

Furthermore, a concerned citizen wanted to do something for the department in my honor, by providing our SWAT team with new weapons to update its arsenal.

CHAPTER EIGHT

Where Do I Go from Here? A Second Chance from "Second Chance"

After my shooting I wrote a letter to Richard Davis who founded Second Chance Body Armor in Central Lake Michigan. The company was then one of the smaller body-armor manufacturers in the country, but it accounted for more officers' lives saved than all of the other companies combined. I didn't expect to hear back. I just wanted to thank the company for providing me with a lifesaving product. Little did I know at the time that this would be the beginning of a long relationship with Second Chance.

A week or so later the company contacted me, asking for my measurements for a new vest. I explained that I could not afford one, at which point they replied that they were giving me a free one to replace the one I was wearing when I was shot, and in addition, one hundred dollars and a pair of shooter's muffs. I learned that this was their common practice for Body Armor vest survivors.

On the heels of receiving my new vest, the company invited Carole and I to Toronto, Canada, to represent them in their booth at that year's International Chiefs of Police (IACP) convention. We both were nervous about the attention we might receive, but we agreed that it would be worth the trip so long as we could share our story for the sake of saving the lives of fellow cops.

At the convention we met other Second Chance "saves," and shared our story with numerous line officers and administrators. As was true of his employees, Richard Davis treated us like family. He had wanted to meet me because I was the first of his "saves" to use a vehicle as a weapon to halt an attack. It was also the first time since the shooting that Carole and I anticipated a respite from the children and a change of scenery.

In 1988, Second Chance invited us to its factory in Central Lake for a reenactment of my shooting for their promotional film "Second Chance Versus Magnum Force," which included the stories of other "saves" whom we befriended at that time, as well as other folks from the company. Our son Sam, born shortly before the filming, traveled with us. While there, the company invited us to attend the 1988 IACP convention in Portland, Oregon.

Because Melissa, our third daughter, was suffering from constant ear infections that year, we weren't comfortable leaving her at home. So Carole figured out a way for the children to blend in with the rest of us in the booth. She made a bib for Sam, imprinted with the headline "Second Chance Save #382½" in recognition of my save-number, and made a pinafore for Melissa with the caption "Second Chance Kid."

As a result, the kids did more than blend in. They became the big draw of the convention as everyone came to see the "Second Chance Kids." Not surprisingly, several months later a rival company produced a poster showing a vested police officer holding a baby. It was a poignant message. Even if the competitor had lifted the idea from us, we did not complain. For there is no copyright for a life destroyed by bullets from a gun.

* * *

In February 1990, Second Chance offered me a position as their factory representative on the East Coast. I would cover the states of Virginia, Maryland, Delaware, New Jersey, West Virginia, Pennsylvania, and the District of Columbia. The job had the potential of being lucrative, and I believed I could sell their Body Armor since I knew first-hand just how well they worked. I thought that for us as a family the opportunity could be a great break from the stress of the prior three years. At the same time, I loved my vocation as a cop. It was so much a part of me that I was reluctant to leave it.

I was still trying to decide what to do when the department experienced another shooting involving officers from both our department and the sheriff's. The case involved a cop-inflicted suicide, (also known as Suicide by Cop) that had gone badly at a local restaurant. Such a suicide typically pertains to persons who wish to commit suicide but are unwilling to inflict it upon themselves. They will force officers to shoot them by luring the officers to a location and then raise a weapon or shoot at officers, thereby forcing a confrontation. In this case two citizens were shot, one of whom was killed by the suspect and the other critically wounded. The suspect then sent out a waitress to call the police. He waited patiently for their arrival and then walked out the front door and raised his weapon towards the responding officers and fired, forcing them to shoot. The suspect died from his injuries.

The deceased employee was the restaurant's swamper. He was shot first. Just about all us officers in the Missoula area knew and liked him because we regularly stopped there for coffee late at night. Whenever he brought out his obnoxiously loud vacuum cleaner, we teasingly threatened to shoot him.

I was called to work early for the day shift and to help at the crime scene so that the night-shift officers involved in the shooting could return to the station to handle their paperwork. On the way there, I fleetingly thought to myself that someone had finally shot the swamper. I was thoroughly shocked when I arrived to find out that he had in fact been killed. I learned that as he was vacuuming the floor past the suspect's booth, the shooter shoved a .44 magnum revolver under the swamper's chin and fired. Death was instantaneous.

When I arrived at the scene, I discovered that three city and two county officers had taken part in the gunfight with the swamper's assailant. Fortunately, none of our officers were injured. The other civilian survived but was in for a long road to recovery. I spoke to the on-scene commander and mentioned to him the importance of debriefing the officers as soon as possible in order to avoid some of the problems that I had experienced. Eventually, I learned that this hadn't happened, and that at least four of them had endured a degree of suffering that could have been alleviated, at least to some extent, had their post-traumatic issues been addressed. While I loved being part of the department, I felt that this was a sign that it was time for me to leave. So I gave notice and left for the East Coast in May 1990.

But that is getting slightly ahead of the story. For we still had a job to do at the scene.

Even though I knew the swamper only casually, it was very traumatic seeing him with his head pretty much blown off, which made it all the more difficult to deliver the death notification later that afternoon, for I had grown up with the swamper's grandson.

* * *

An interesting side to the investigation emerged as Detective Rusty Wickman searched for the fatal bullet that killed the swamper. Removing the ceiling tile that the bullet had penetrated, he could see where the bullet had hit a truss. He asked for my flashlight and, while surveying the ceiling light hanging from the neighboring tile, he noticed a dark spot within the globe of the bulb.

Upon closer inspection, he discovered that after the .44 magnum bullet had passed through the victim's head, it continued upward into the truss from which it ricocheted and then angled downwards, passed through the light fixture, and gutted the receptacle and the screw-end of the light bulb before coming to rest inside the globe without breaking the glass. The path of that bullet could not be reproduced in a million years.

* * *

Subsequent to this incident, when the time arrived to leave for the East Coast, I "laid out the fleece," as Gideon did,[1] asking the Lord to do two things before we left. The first was to see my dad receive Christ into his life. The second was to obtain an offer on our house. Indeed, within the next few weeks both requests were granted. However, the deal on our house fell through the day before we were to leave. I could not argue with God. For I had not prayed specifically for it to sell, if, in fact, that was what God expected of me. Putting God to the test is always a precarious undertaking. Even so, the house sold the first day we were on the road to Virginia, which was the geographical center of my territory. Thus it all worked out.

Over the next three years I became the jack of all trades and the master of none. The position with Second Chance proved to me that I was a cop but not a salesman. After eight months of traveling and attempting to build a solid customer base, I was basically broke. Come January 1990 I decided to pass my territory on to another representative. So Second Chance flew me down to their annual meeting in Orlando, Florida, to complete the transition. However, a funny thing happened on the way to the handover.

After taking a taxi to the hotel, I needed to walk approximately two blocks to my room. With my luggage and Second Chance's gear in hand, this wasn't an easy task. It was an unseasonable warm January day and extremely humid. I was wearing a suit that was soaked with perspiration by the time I arrived at the room. I unlocked the door and scooted through it, dropping my belongings on a chair. When I turned around, I noticed an unmade bed with skimpy women's lingerie lying on it. A visual inspection of the room revealed the presence of ladies makeup and toiletries.

While Second Chance had been very good to me and quite generous, this was a bit over the top, even for them. What on earth had they done?

When I had arrived at the airport, I had spoken with Carole who was at home with our four children. So I ruled her out as a possibility, and I backed out of the room. I carried my heap of bags

---

[1] See the Hebrew book of Judges 6:33–40.

the two blocks back to the hotel office, where I was advised by an insistent desk clerk that I must be mistaken. I assured him that I was not mistaken, but he insisted that we return to the room to recheck it. When we got there, to his amazement, someone was in the room. He asked, and I assured him, that it was not my wife. I concluded that he must have originally come from the "Show Me State" of Missouri. What I needed at that point was to be shown to a new room.

For the next six months, I conducted internal investigations and did surveillance work for a local auto parts company based in Merrifield, Virginia, with locations in Virginia, Washington, DC, Pennsylvania, and West Virginia. Thereafter I drove a sales route for the same company, a job that suddenly ended one weekend when its owners decided to reorganize. When eight other guys and I came to work on Monday, we learned that our jobs had been eliminated as a cost-saving measure. With nothing more than a week's severance pay in hand, and finding myself unemployed for the first time in my married life, I yearned to return to law-enforcement.

Shortly after being laid off by the auto parts company, I replied to an ad from a company in Washington, DC, seeking to hire uniformed diplomatic security officers for the United States Department of State. Once my application was processed, I participated in its five-week training academy before joining the force.

I said "force," but "farce" would be a better word to describe the job. From the time I went to work at "State," until quitting about six months later, all I could say was that it was the sorriest outfit I had ever worked for. Whenever they let you do the job you were supposed to do, it wasn't so bad. The company's officers and line supervisors were decent people, but its senior management was corrupt. A year or two after I departed, I learned that the company had lost its contract and was being sued and investigated by the government. It seemed that it intentionally looked for reasons to fire people or to make their lives so miserable that they quit. The owners made money off of the academy classes, so they kept grinding them out, only to repeat the process after forcing more employees to leave.

I spent the remainder of my time in Fairfax, Virginia, employed by a window company owned by one of my friends at church. While I enjoyed working with my hands, it simply wasn't my cup of tea, even though I quickly moved up to a customer service position. I remained there until I returned to Montana in May 1993.

* * *

Spiritually speaking, our time in Virginia was one of great growth for our family. Northern Virginia and Washington, DC, were among the most expensive areas in the country. We lived from paycheck to paycheck, but we never starved. Our life as a couple grew exponentially from the teaching and preaching at Fairfax Baptist Temple, and we made a number of lifelong friends.
We learned to trust God in all things.

One Sunday in particular stood out for us as a family. During the morning service the pastor announced that the congregation would be taking up a food offering that evening for a needy family. I was between jobs right after being laid off by the auto parts company, and we were down to our last twenty dollars.

During the service, the Lord impressed upon my heart our need to participate in the offering. Yet, I wavered well into the early afternoon, trying to reconcile in my mind how we could help the needy family and at the same time support our own family that week on twenty dollars.

Carole and I prayed about the matter after we went home. We knew that contributing to the offering was what we were supposed to do. So I watched the kids that afternoon while Carole went out and spent those last twenty dollars on groceries for the recipient family.

That evening at church we both felt a deep sense of peace, believing that everything would work out. Above all, we were glad that our twenty dollars would be a blessing for someone else.

At the conclusion of the service, I was talking with some friends in the hallway when the pastor walked up to me and put his hand on my shoulder. He said that the food offering was for us. I stood there totally dumbfounded. How did he possibly know that we were in need? Somehow he had found out. He then walked me to the back doors of the church. There sat fourteen bags of groceries. We were shocked.

At that very moment, I saw a Christian brother by the name of Arabaldo Decovalo walking down the hall. His family was every bit as needy as mine. So I spoke to him and told him about the groceries, and said that we wanted his family to take half of them. Pulling up behind the church, and without looking into the bags, Arabaldo took seven and I took seven.

When we arrived home that night and began unpacking the bags with the children, we noted that all of us had found our favorite treats in the bags. Each one of the kids received a favorite cereal, and not a single thing was something that we would not have eaten.

In addition, the items Carole had purchased that afternoon were also there. We were literally in tears as we finished unpacking. Among the treats were those we hadn't been able to afford in ages.

I called Arabaldo to share the news. When he answered, he said that first he had something he wanted to share with me. He recounted the very same experience we had just had. Arabaldo and his family were from Brazil. In their bags they found their favorite ethnic foods and treats for everyone in his family.

Nobody had any idea that I had given half of the food offering to Arabaldo and his family. Until I had seen him in the hallway and remembered his struggles, the thought hadn't crossed my mind to do it. When the people of the congregation gave their offerings that day, they had no idea as to who would be the recipients of the groceries. But God surely knew, and that is what mattered.

There were many times that God showed us his grace and goodness during our time at Fairfax Baptist Temple, by taking care of our needs in miraculous ways, which someday may become the subject of another book.

It may seem crazy that we would leave such a wonderful church and its people, but the whole time we were in Virginia it did not feel like home, either for Carole or for me. We both felt drawn back to Montana, even though neither of us truly understood why.

The move was a hard one because we were leaving her parents and brothers again, and yet we knew it was the right move for us to make at the time.

* * *

My Dad drove out from Montana to help us pack for the move. Inadvertently, he taught me a lesson that I am occasionally reminded of still today.

We were packing up the last items from our bedroom closet to stow in the moving truck. Dad had already commented about all the things we had accumulated, and he noted the large quantity of shoes on Carole's side of the closet. He asked me why a woman needed so many shoes.

Being a practical guy, I said, "You know, I really don't know. I would think that one pair in each color should be sufficient."

Clearly, those words did not represent one of my finer moments. For we threw a copious number of shoes away in order to finish the packing. I was so proud of myself for making a command decision and was certain that Dad was proud of me as well.

Things were busy the next day. So I failed to mention my bold decision to my lovely bride. That was probably a good thing, because she may have divorced me and sent me packing right then and there if she had known about it before we took off for Montana. But once we arrived in Montana, at least she couldn't leave me quite so easily.

After arriving in Missoula, as Carole and I and my dad were unpacking our closet items, Carole wanted to know where the rest of her shoes were. You could have heard a pin drop when I told her about my great idea.

And did Dad back me up? Not a chance, the traitor! He threw me under the bus and made a speedy exit from the room when he saw how mad his daughter-in-law was.

Husbands young and old could gain something from my fiasco. Under no circumstances should they throw out their wives' shoes. For all I know, the action could well be a felony on the books in all states and territories of the United States, and in Washington, DC. Wives may not be so merciful as to drop the charges, either.

My belief is that all women's shoes should come with a warning label:

"Men, beware! Under penalty of public flogging or the torture of the rack, thou shalt not touch thy wife's shoes nor give a single thought to throwing them away."

* * *

By May 1993 we had gotten pretty good at being gypsies. So we decided that this move would be our last. We were tired of moving. Yet, little did we know how far from the last our last move would be.

Once in Missoula, I landed a job at the Axman Discount Center. Axman was truly a guy's store. It sold everything from railroad ties to guns and plenty in-between. I worked there for the next year while I went through the process of joining the Montana Highway Patrol.

During that time we lived with my parents. We had planned to find a place of our own, but Dad persuaded us to stay put until I was hired for the new Highway Patrol position. What we thought would be a few weeks turned into more than a year and a half.

This turned out to be a blessing, for it meant that we were with my mother in June 1994 when my father died. The Friday before he died, I discovered that I would enter the Highway Patrol Academy in July.

The Sunday of Dad's death I spent a bittersweet day at the hospital with him. He was recovering from a heart attack and we were hoping he would gain enough strength for a second by-pass surgery. I planned on going to church that morning with my family, but the Lord impressed upon me the need to spend time with Dad. We talked all day. He shared with me things that he had never shared before. I did not realize it at the time, but looking back, I believe he knew that his time was short.

After returning home that evening, I had just gone to bed when the hospital called to say he had taken a turn for the worse. I returned to the hospital in time to see him as they rolled him into the cardiac catheterization lab. We spoke "I love you" to one another. I hugged him and said I would see him when he got out. But something in his eyes told me that he knew it was the last time I would see him on this earth. I prayed that it would not be so, yet in my heart I knew it was true.

When across the intercom I heard the summons of "code blue" for the cath lab, my worst fear materialized. While that Sunday was one of the hardest days of my life, I will always be grateful that God had spared my father for those few years prior to our losing him and impressed upon me the need to be at his side during the last day of his life.

Don Schultz was a leader, a helper to those in need, and a friend to many. He was a devoted husband and a loving and generous father and grandfather who adored his grandchildren. His manner of life exemplified for me how to be a man. Simply put, my dad was my hero.

People stood in the foyer and on the front steps of the church during his funeral service, for which there was standing room only—a true testament to his character and to the good life that he led.

When I, too, take flight from this world, I shall look forward to seeing him yet again, among all the saints who from their labors rest.

My sister Connie, my brothers Kenny and Brian, and I, all of us, had the task of cleaning out my parents' house when Mom decided to sell it several months later. During that process, while clearing out the attic and Dad's garage, I discovered that he was every bit the pack rat that the rest of us were.

To think of it! He had the nerve not to back me up when Carole discovered what he and I had done with her shoes!

One day, when I too get to Heaven, Dad and I are going to discuss the matter!

CHAPTER NINE

Starting Over and Fast Becoming the World's Oldest Rookie

In July 1994 I entered the Montana Highway Patrol Academy class of recruits at the ripe old age of thirty-five. I discovered that it was going to take a lot of effort on my part if I wanted to do well in relation to all of the youngsters just beginning their careers. Like the rest, I was classified as a temporary employee. I was motivated to succeed by the fact that graduation determined eligibility for full-time employment. Even then we were placed on a waiting list until someone left the department. At the time of my matriculation there were but two immediate departmental openings.

My mother had just decided to put her house on the market, so I also needed to do well in order to support my family and obtain a place for us all to live. But how likely was it, given the academy pay of $7.00 an hour?

I knew I was faced with an uphill challenge. But if there was one thing I had learned from my father, it was the determination to do whatever it takes to support the family. My mother graciously purchased me a word processor, which was a cross between a typewriter and a computer. (For those youngsters who don't know what a typewriter is, Webster's dictionary or Google will provide a definition.)

I knew I'd probably be academically competitive, given as much hands-on experience as I had already had. I was more concerned with my physical fitness for keeping up with my classmates. My fears were allayed, however, when I discovered that the academy used the Cooper Test which contained age-appropriate exercises graded on a sliding scale. It afforded old buzzards like me a flying chance at more than just winging it. Whoever Mr. Cooper was, I suspect he understood the adage that age and treachery triumph over youthful exuberance every time. If not, then I could surely correct him.

During the next twelve weeks I studied harder than ever. When the "kids" at the academy were playing cards I was typing the day's notes with my word processor and printing them. When they were sleeping in I was either at the gym or running outdoors every other morning. One of the kids, Jason Davis, was doing the same. Even though he was a youngster, he was as dedicated as I. When graduation day came that November, Jason graduated as first in the class and I as second. His grade average had beaten mine by a quarter of one point. We both were stationed in Missoula after patrol school. Jason became a member of our family for the next several months. He moved in with us until he married his lovely bride, Sherry.

* * *

I did learn a thing or two in the academy. It was by far the best firearms training I had ever had. By the time I completed it, I was confident when using my Smith and Wesson 9-mm pistol, my M-14 rifle, and my Remington 870 shotgun. With the latter I had bruises to show for it. We spent hours on the range and shot thousands of rounds. For a gun nut like me it was as though Christmas had come early.

As part of those exercises, the FBI brought in a firearms training simulator (FATS) that provided a prerecorded series of "shoot and don't shoot" scenarios with which to interact with our firearms. At the conclusion of my session I had aced the course, so the instructor asked me to come and talk with him. He said, "You were either trigger happy or you have been involved in a shooting before. Which was it?" I explained that I had been in more than one shooting and also had been shot. He suspected as much because I was so quick to recognize threats and to decipher which ones were valid targets. He furthermore said that officers previously involved in shootings generally reacted as I did. To me that was a compliment, although I was happy enough to have passed the course without shooting grandma.

Sadly, I don't recall the name of the academy's accident investigation instructor. I would not have graduated without him. I had passed first and second level algebra in high school by the skin of my teeth. But I had never understood a real-world application for it until I studied accident investigation, when for the first time it made sense to me. The instructor returned every evening on his own time to bring lamebrains like me up to speed. I will be forever grateful to him for his selfless willingness to teach us what he clearly loved.

Even though I had endured the effects of tear gas and pepper spray more times than I care to remember in the military, in the police academies, and on the street, we still had to suffer through the drills in patrol school. The theory behind the training was twofold. First, it was important to know how to get through the experience if we ever happened to get sprayed. Second, after discovering the painfulness of it, we would think twice before using it on someone else.

Just about every time pepper spray is employed, there is the likelihood of being hit with it by a partner while seeking to gain control of a crowd or handcuff a suspect. The reality check for inflicting the nasty stuff consists of assessing the length to which a potential recipient may go in refusing to cooperate, including the situation in which an officer is engaged in a full-fledged physical fight with a suspect. In either case, it rarely ends well for the lead officer, the other officers, or the suspect.

When the day arrived for the live rehearsal, I was chosen to be the first to be sprayed. The instructors set up a scenario in which I was to undertake a traffic stop of some instructors who were role-playing as the bad guys. I was told to expect to be sprayed with actual pepper spray sometime during the encounter, and I was to respond with an inert canister containing water and compressed air. But instead of providing me with an inert canister, the instructors decided to play a prank upon their role-playing counterparts by giving me a canister containing the real deal.

As I conducted the stop, the driver suddenly produced a canister of pepper spray and sprayed me. I returned the favor, but it was not with water and compressed air. Consequently, all involved suffered the joys of experiencing a dose of oleoresin capsicum, the scientific name for pepper spray. Incidentally, Trooper Bryan Adams happened to be the driver during my scenario. We had attended Missoula's Hellgate High School together. So in that respect the prank was a treat for me, albeit a painful one for both of us!

Those who have undergone the pepper-spray ritual understand that it is a gift of pain that keeps giving. For those who haven't undergone it, let's just say that the best description I've heard is that it is like the worst possible sunburn rubbed with sand paper. The lungs feel as though they are inhaling the vapor of a fire-breathing dragon, and the eyeballs react as if being stabbed with a thousand needles. Whoever invented the substance was a true sadist.

After concluding the role-playing demonstration, I had the added pleasure of helping to decontaminate the rest of the class who, I might add, were all good fighters. If you can imagine the stinging effect of a single drop of Joy dish liquid in your eyeballs, then imagine the excruciating discomfort of washing your eyes out repeatedly with Joy in order to cleanse them of the pepper spray. You don't just sneeze and hack up hair balls. You emit long streams of mucus from your mouth and nose.

After cleansing myself and my peers, I falsely believed that I would no longer feel like a human torch afire. But when I went to bed that night and put my arm beneath the pillow, I felt a sudden need to call the fire department. I also was keenly aware of the screams of pain emitting from the showers that night as my academy mates rinsed off. The law of gravity sent water streaming over the tiny droplets of oleoresin capsicum trapped inside their freshly opened pores, reactivating the pain. It was enough to make a mute monkey scream out loud.

* * *

After patrol school, Jason and I received our field assignments and were on our way to Missoula. The last obstacle to be overcome was the field training itself, which we requested to be close to home. But the Montana Highway Patrol was like most government agencies, assigning us to the hinterlands, which in our case was eastern Montana. It was about as far from Missoula as you could get.

We were to train with the same field training officers (FTOs) but to rotate back and forth between posts, with our longest time spent with the primary FTO and our shortest time with the secondary FTO. The final week we were to be with our primary officer again to either being employed by the highway patrol or altogether eliminated.

I was assigned to Trooper Keith Edgell of Billings, Montana, as my primary officer. Jason was assigned to someone whom I shall refer to as Trooper Micro, who was just that, a micro manager. He was stationed in a small town in eastern Montana next to the North Dakota border.   Trooper Edgell was a great field training officer. He respected my previous experience even though I asked him not to consider it. I was new with the department and did not want to be treated differently than the other rookies. We got along well and I learned the idiosyncrasies of being a trooper as opposed to a city or county police officer. The Montana Highway Patrol is primarily a traffic safety unit. We investigated accidents, patrolled the highways assisting stranded motorists, worked traffic to reduce accidents, and backed up local city and county officers when necessary.

When the initial phase of field training was over, Jason and I met in the Billings office before heading home for our days off. Jason was a nervous wreck, concerned about passing the FTO phase. I had watched Jason through our time together at the academy and was confident that he would be an excellent officer. I told him that things couldn't possibly be that bad, that he was overreacting and needed to calm down, and that everything would be fine. But I could not have been more mistaken. The first day that I worked with Trooper Micro I discovered just how mistaken I really was.

From having talked with Trooper Edgell, Trooper Micro knew that I was an experienced officer. He also knew that I had been doing fine under Edgell's training. As with Edgell, I advised Micro that I wanted to learn the Highway Patrol's way of doing things. It was during my very first traffic stop that I realized that I was in for a very long few weeks with Trooper Micro, and that I owed Jason an apology.

Trooper Micro and I stopped a car for speeding. I approached from the driver's side just as I had done literally hundreds of times before. In all of my previous field training, the training officer had assumed a backup position on the passenger side of the vehicle. But not Trooper Micro: He followed me to the driver's side and stood over my shoulder. As I spoke to the violator, Micro began kicking my right foot. I ignored him until I completed my contact and returned to the patrol car. Trooper Micro then asked if I knew why he had kicked me and I said that I didn't. He explained that my right foot could have been run over if the driver had pulled away quickly.

I could not believe what I was hearing. I had bladed my body in an angle to the vehicle, as taught. I had stood behind the rear door post, as taught. And I remained in a modified interview stance to allow a quick reaction if need be. This was the way I had been trained in the 1978 and 1982 police academies, as well as in the 1994 patrol school. So, at first I thought he was kidding. The distraction he caused by kicking me while I was speaking to the driver was actually more dangerous than the chance of my foot being run over.

As I thought about it, I said to myself, Here's a small-town guy who hasn't made a fraction of the arrests or traffic stops that I have made, and he's worried about my foot placement? Really?

I could not figure out whether he was just plain arrogant or whether he was somehow intimidated by my experience, which I continued to play down. He seemed to relish criticizing everything I did and was quick to belittle me in public, and around fellow officers which was not indicative of a good supervisor or training officer.

The next time I saw Trooper Edgell, he noted that I was on edge. So had Jason been on edge when he arrived for his second phase of training. So I profusely apologized to Jason for not having taken seriously his experience with Trooper Micro.

Jason and I both passed field training, and yet those weeks with Micro were surely among the worst of our careers. I sincerely hoped that somehow Micro might become more human. When he was later promoted to sergeant, I quietly thanked God that he was not transferred to my district.

* * *

Two notable accidents occurred in Billings during my field training. The first took place on a Sunday morning at the base of a narrow country road midway between two hills. I was struck by the fact that a mere few seconds determined the difference between life and death. If the drivers had come upon one another from opposite directions a second or two later than they did, they would have seen each other. But that was not the case.

A sizable SUV, occupied by a large family, collided head-on with a small truck driven by a teenager on his way to hunt. The teen had done everything right. He was restrained by a seat belt and he was not speeding. Yet sometimes it just isn't a person's lucky day. His small pickup was no match for the larger SUV. So a promising young life was snuffed out because of the difference that a few seconds made. Some of the children in the third seat of the SUV were not restrained. One of them flew forward, landing on the front floorboard, suffering only minor injuries.

Over the next three years I was repeatedly reminded of the importance of seatbelts. I watched people crawl out of wrecks that by all accounts would have been fatalities, but for the seatbelts. On the flip side, I saw many an accident that should have resulted in minor injuries but incurred serious ones or worse.

The second notable accident involved a drunk driver in a pickup. Had he been wearing a seatbelt, he would have likely died, for his was a rollover accident in which the driver's-side roof completely caved in, leaving him but a small space for escape.

The anti-seatbelt folks do well not to exclaim that seatbelts kill people. Out of the hundreds of accidents I have seen, only two accidents where unrestrained drivers would have been killed had they been wearing a seat belt.

Flying into the windshield or outside the vehicle at the speed that the vehicles is traveling increases the odds of making a quick trip to heaven or hell.

The safe bet is to buckle up.

CHAPTER TEN

On The Road Again, Chasing Taillights and Encountering Tragedy

Our Missoula District sergeant was Sean Driscoll, one of the finest supervisors for whom I ever worked. He was quickly promoted up the chain and before retiring became the chief of the Montana Highway Patrol. He was a caring, by-the-book, fair supervisor. Not only so, but he was a friend and trusted confidant when needed. I was blessed and honored to serve under him.

As I have said about the importance of wearing seatbelts, a case in point involved a pickup truck towing a trailer on a very cold and icy winter morning. The vehicle was traveling at a low speed on a mountainous county road. As it rounded a curve it slid off the shoulder and rolled over at least twice as it tumbled down a snowy embankment before landing upright. The snow was deep enough to slow and cushion the vehicle, yet the unrestrained driver suffered a broken neck that left him as a quadriplegic. Had he been wearing a seatbelt, he likely wouldn't have been so much as even bruised. There wasn't a single scratch or dent on the vehicle.

Police officers drive thousands of miles per year. It goes without saying that, regardless of how good at driving, an officer will eventually be involved in a wreck. During my time with the patrol, my only accident occurred on Montana Highway 93 in a small placed called Lolo, the site of Traveler's Rest State Park. A sheriff's deputy had been dispatched to a domestic disturbance just a couple of miles from my location. His department's backup was farther out, so I advised the dispatcher that I would assist.

Traffic was light, so I made the mistake of checking my mirrors, but without doing an over-the-shoulder check. As I pulled around the shoulder of the road, and swung out to make a U-turn, an Isuzu Trooper (which was a vehicle, not an officer) was in my blind spot. I clipped its rear fender as it passed me. Suddenly everything went into slow motion. I watched the Isuzu rocking from side to side before the force of gravity finally flipped it over on its side. I remember thinking, "No!" to myself and wishing I could push it back onto its wheels. Clearly, I was at fault, and luckily no one was hurt.

Upon his arrival at the scene of the accident, Sergeant Driscoll's reaction was memorable. He didn't ask what happened. He simply asked if I was okay. Only after we had completed our work did he counsel me about being more careful. The fact that he was genuinely concerned for my welfare went a long way. Supervisors from other departments had not exhibited the same compassion.

Camaraderie among cops comes with good humor. For humor is one of the characteristics we wear like a badge to face whatever comes our way. While our humor can be a bit morbid at times, it serves as a coping mechanism. Enjoyable practical jokes are rampant. Whenever the chips are down, we are there for each other to protect one another's backs, even if at times we squabble like a dysfunctional family.

At our district office we kept a special traveling trophy, lovingly referred to as the Captain Crunch Award. It was a marvel of pure beauty—a bowling trophy scrounged from a seedy second-hand store, with an empty Captain Crunch cereal box attached. It was awarded to whoever had the most recent accident. That person would then pass it on with great fanfare to its next recipient. I guess I had earned it fairly and squarely. Fortunately, I was able to pass it on within a week or so to one of my academy partners, Kevin Fifield, when he struck a culvert in the median as he sought to turn toward a speeding vehicle.

My patrol car was in the shop for a couple of weeks as a result of my accident. This meant that I was subjected to driving a fleet car. While as a whole they were generally serviceable, the driver's door had sprung on the one I was driving. I had no idea how dangerous a sprung door could be, but I was about to find out.

I was conducting a routine traffic stop on a vehicle that had just run a red light, when it turned onto a side street. My patrol car leaned somewhat to its passenger side as I came to a stop on a slight incline. As I kept an eye on the violator, I gave my door a slight kick to open it completely in order to exit the car. (Note to myself: This is a bad idea when the car has a sprung door and is sitting on an incline.)

As quickly as I kicked the door open and stepped forward, the law of physics took over. For when an object in motion suddenly hits its apex and reverses course, it returns at roughly the same velocity that triggered it in the first place. (I should have paid more attention in my high school physics class.)

As I stepped out, the door traveled back at me like a boxer's roundhouse punch, colliding with the left side of my head at the temple. The blow knocked me back into my seat from which I saw the proverbial stars of heaven. I can attest to the fact that such stars are no urban legend. For I was a bit fuzzy for a few minutes before I could compose myself enough to continue the traffic stop. Fortunately, the door hit me in the part of my head that my wife purports to be rather hard. Otherwise, I may have been killed.

Regrettably, my eyes were not as resilient as my head. Six months later I went for a routine eye exam and discovered that I had a partially detached retina. The doctor described the injury as a boxer's injury commonly caused by blows to the temple region. He asked if in the last several months someone had hit me in the temple. I said no but then remembered the door incident. He agreed that it was likely the culprit. So I had laser surgery that week to repair the retina. Once again God was looking out for me.

* * *

That experience is a story in itself. While I'm glad that the physician saved my eye, I came away believing that this surgery could perhaps become an official means of punishment in our penal system, as well as a technique for interrogating terrorists. If that were so, I'm confident we would have fewer criminals and would-be terrorists on the streets.

The doctor preps you for the procedure by explaining that you need to be awake during the surgery and that it will not be painful.

In my experience, any time a doctor says that a procedure is not going to be painful, then things are likely not to end well. The doctor's idea of pain and patient's idea of pain are derived from entirely different perspectives.

I knew that I was in trouble when they strapped me down in a chair and locked my head into a contraption that was surely used as a form of torture during the Middle Ages. It had been sufficiently modernized so as to look harmless enough, that is, until they strapped me into it.

Once I was securely positioned, the nurse told me that she was putting numbing drops in my eyes to alleviate pain.

"Pain from what?" I asked!

"Pain from the needle," she said.

"Needles, did you say? I don't remember anyone saying anything about needles."

"Oh, yes," she said nonchalantly. "It's the one we poke in your eye to administer the anesthesia."

Let me simply say for the record that there is nothing quite like observing a needle coming straight for your eye when you are trussed up like a Christmas goose, with a medieval gadget propping your eyelid open and a doctor telling you not to move your eye.

"Don't move, you say?"

I was still too busy wondering why I had not run like a rabbit when they began strapping me in the contraption like the fictional Hannibal Lecter, the serial killer. I had never liked horror movies to begin with. At this very moment I knew exactly why.

Then the paralyzing thought crossed my mind that my eyeball might suddenly pop like a balloon. Surely this procedure will dissuade criminals and terrorists everywhere from wanting to do time to deserve our penal system.

While I survived to tell the story, even now my eye twitches uncontrollably whenever I see a needle. I have God to thank that my sight is still good and that there is little chance I will take up a life of cops and robbers in which I am the robber.

* * *

Some people are slow learners. After stopping a vehicle for a DUI one night, I processed the belligerent driver at the scene and then once again at the station. He was an arrogant and overall unpleasant fellow.

The jail was full at the time, so he called his wife to come and get him. But something told me that he would go directly to his vehicle and drive it. So as soon as she picked him up at the station, I took a different route to his car to see if I were right. And sure enough, I watched him stagger over to it and crawl behind the wheel. Then as he prepared to drive off, I pulled in and stopped him.

He got what he had asked for, which was a second DUI arrest that very same night. A very unhappy two-timer was awarded first-class accommodations at the Missoula County Bastille. It was not the first time I encountered such arrogance, nor was it the last.

The book of Proverbs takes note of a recidivist's sin. "As a dog returns to his vomit, so a fool returns to his folly" (Prov 26:11). Once again, the Bible sets forth an apt metaphor.

* * *

Within the expanse of Missoula and the surrounding counties it was common for us to be called to successive accidents that had occurred at considerable distances from one another. I recall one particular morning when I traveled almost ninety miles between two vehicular wrecks.

On another occasion, an Easter Sunday afternoon, I received a call to go after a drunk driver in the North end of the county. My partner and I traveled 110 miles before we caught up with the driver and arrested her.

On still another occasion, under a mutual aid agreement, the Idaho State Police requested that I respond to a remote motorcycle wreck. I drove over 100 miles to reach it, which was an even greater distance than the local Idaho trooper would have had to travel.

Long distances meant that we were more prone to encounter unexpected developments along the way. The Idaho State Department of Transportation meant business, though, when it posted roadside warning signs in the Idaho Panhandle. If a sign stated that the speed limit was thirty-five miles per hour on a curve, then we cops had better not be going thirty-six miles per hour or we might find ourselves cascading over the edge and plunging into the river far below.

Fortunately for me, the traffic was light on one particular night that I vividly recall. As I rounded a curve and accelerated, I noticed that the road itself appeared to move. So I dropped my speed. Suddenly, a herd of several hundred elk appeared leisurely crossing the road. Before I could continue, it took a good five minutes for them to clear themselves from the highway.

* * *

One cloudy afternoon an all-points bulletin to every unit flashed across my radio, concerning an armed carjacking at a shopping center. The suspect was driving a white SUV that had just turned off of Missoula's Reserve Street and onto the interstate highway, when suddenly it appeared directly in front of my zone partner's car and mine.

Already in the lead, my zone partner led the pursuit. By the time we reached the Turah exit several miles east, police cars were converging from every direction. Even the county sheriff, Doug Chase, was coming our way.

Without warning, the car-jacker veered off onto the exit ramp. My partner, who was too close behind him to make the turn, overshot the exit. So for a few seconds I took the lead. The car-jacker, driving all too fast in his approach to the local frontage road, sped up onto the opposite ramp and promptly lost control. What followed was the most spectacular real-time crash I had ever witnessed.

The vehicle side-slipped towards the median and then did a complete end-over-end tumble before flipping onto its side and rolling over for yet another two revolutions. As its windows shattered, broken glass and the contents of the vehicle scattered across the median. The suspect, a fourteen-year-old, received only minor injuries despite not wearing his seatbelt. The gun he used during the carjacking was found among the debris in the median. His accomplices were caught in a separate pursuit in Missoula.

Despite all the odds against human survival, it seemed that God once again looked out for drunks, fools, and even criminals who do everything possible to skirt the rules of the road and the law of gravity.

* * *

Divine intervention, I have repeatedly discovered, however, is not to be minimized. I vividly recall the night I was working on the DUI team with my counterpart, Deputy Phil Tillman of the Missoula County Sheriff's Department.

We were sitting in a parking lot at Third and Russell Streets, discussing our strategy for the night. (If you're a cop, you're undoubtedly thinking that we were sitting there, door-to-door in our cars, simply shooting the breeze, although we were actually strategizing.)

As we talked, we both heard a terrific crash and looked towards the adjacent parking lot. A car had appeared out of nowhere, first crashing onto Third Street and then bouncing into the parking lot of a supermarket. Being but a hundred yards from us, our response was quick.

As we pulled up to the vehicle containing two front-seat males and two rear-seat females, I observed what appeared to be a pipe protruding through the passenger side of the windshield. It appeared to have impaled the person sitting on the right front passenger side.

This isn't going to be pretty, I thought to myself.

The pipe had also struck the rear-passenger female in the side of her forehead, causing a significant circular laceration.

We called dispatch to summons fire and ambulance personnel to the scene.

All four passengers—young kids—lay unconscious. All four had suffered broken backs. Yet, astonishingly, none were paralyzed.

The passenger who appeared to have been impaled was blessed beyond measure. The pipe had slid from his hand up through his jacket sleeve and out the armpit of the jacket, leaving only minor contusions. Had the pipe been another three to four inches to the left, it would have skewered him like a human shish kabob.

It turned out that the car had been speeding along a street in the neighborhood above Third Street. The driver, being drunk, was unable to see the dead-end barrier in front of him, which he sheared off before going airborne, first behind and then beside an apartment building. The vehicle flew at least twenty-five feet into the air before descending and striking an eight-foot, chain-link fence bearing the pole that penetrated the windshield. As the car came to rest in the parking lot, it bounced, dragging a section of the fence beneath its undercarriage.

Needless to say, the driver's DUI was not contested at court. I suspect that lawsuits brought by the passengers were of far more concern to him than the DUI itself.

But here's the irony of what was a terribly bad decision to drive when drunk. Had the car's occupants been sober, bracing themselves against the catastrophe, then most likely some of them, if not all, would have died. As it was, their drunken stupor left their bodies lax and flexible.

Was the grace of God at work? Would anyone like to claim otherwise?

* * *

I don't know what it is about Sundays, but things seem to happen to me more often on Sundays than any other day.

I had been sent to Mineral County to cover for an officer who was off duty. As I worked the radar along Interstate 90 about forty miles from the Idaho border, a black Corvette screamed past me at 120 miles per hour. So I hit the highway, trailing it.

It took me four miles to get close. Thankfully, due to a series of S-curves, the driver couldn't drive worth beans. But as soon as I gained enough ground to stop him, he took off again. At the speeds we were traveling, we would soon reach the Idaho border. So I asked dispatch to notify the Idaho State Police that we were coming and that I needed stop-sticks set up on the road at the top of the pass.

Just before reaching the border I lost sight of the suspect. When I arrived at the state line the Idaho troopers were waiting with their stop-sticks. They quickly advised me that the suspect had not yet come by. So I turned back, drove to the closest exit, and pulled off the road, where I found a couple of old fellas fishing off of a bridge. As I pulled up to them, they asked if I was hunting a black Corvette. I said, "Yes," and they said, We, kinda figured you'd be back. He went up that logging road, but you needn't worry because he won't get far." I thanked them and continued up the road.

Within minutes I discovered what they meant. The road was extremely rutted and in places I was already bottoming out. As I rounded a curve, there stood the Corvette abandoned in the middle of the road.

After checking it out, I got on my public address mike and announced, "Hey, driver of the black Corvette! You'd best come back to your car because the tow truck is on its way, and it's twenty-five miles back to town. It will be dark in an hour or two, and there are some mighty unfriendly critters in these mountains at night."

With that, a fella popped up from behind a rock about forty yards up the mountainside, and hollered, "What are you going to tow it for?"

I told him to come down and we would discuss it.

It turned out that the driver was an engineer with the Ford Motor Company. Not only so, but he had been the one to design the airbags in our Crown Victoria police cars.

Montana law allowed us to take bond money in lieu of making an arrest on a traffic charge. His bond came to $1,300.00, which he peeled off of a roll of cash from his wallet after I searched his car to be sure he wasn't carrying drugs.

By handing over the bond money, I was obligated to release him to return for a later court date. He never appeared and his bond was forfeited his driving record showed charges of reckless driving, eluding an officer, and speeding.

I never saw him again.

* * *

Easter is day that seems to haunt me. During a stop along Highway 93 South, one Easter evening, I nearly became a hood ornament on a Cadillac. While that may have been a distinct honor, I simply couldn't picture my pudgy little body permanently affixed to such a fine automobile.

I was taking down information from the driver of a car I had stopped, when I heard the Cadillac approaching me from behind. I had nowhere to go, so I hugged the side of the car I had stopped and hoped for the best. It was exceedingly awkward to be cuddling up to a vehicle I hardly knew, but I was out of all other options.

The driver of the Cadillac was drunk and likely had been attracted to my patrol car's lights, which is a common anomaly among drunk drivers. Like bugs drawn to a bug light, they seem unable to help themselves. Fortunately for me, the Cadillac brushed my backside without squashing me between the two vehicles.

The driver and the passenger of the car I had stopped surely must have thought I was a goner, or at least had hoped for as much in order to avoid a citation. Thankfully, they agreed to stay and make a statement to another officer who was heading their way while I took off after the drunk driver in the Cadillac.

Mr. Jackpot, we shall call him, eventually pulled over for me on Reserve Street. He had previously been a multi-DUI offender. His blood alcohol level was more than twice the legal limit of 0.10 percent at the time I stopped him. To his credit, he said that I would have made a lousy accessory to his Cadillac, had he upended me.

On that we both agreed!

* * *

Whenever inclement winter weather hit, it was common for troopers to be snowed in their residences precisely when they were most needed on the road. After all, a Ford Crown Victoria was not a four-wheel drive automobile.

We received twenty-four inches of snow one year, all within the brief span from Christmas Eve to Christmas morning. I spent most of the night clearing my driveway so I could get out at daybreak to go to work. On the whole, I did a great job of it except for the fact that I had failed to consider the road in front of my house.

When I got up Christmas morning, I was thoroughly blocked by the snow's accumulation on the road. Being the dedicated and arguably stupid trooper that I was, I elected to be plowed out. So I contacted my Uncle Herman who put his snow plow to the road.

Once I got to the main highway I was relieved to find that it was fairly clear. But then, after having patted myself on the back for my dedication, I discovered that I was the only trooper within five counties to be on the road that day.

So, Merry Christmas to Trooper Schultz for his ardent devotion.;That's what true dedication sometimes gets you!

* * *

As I've said, I liked to work street patrol because I never knew what I might find in the course of a day. There were times, though, that I came upon situations that I definitely wish I hadn't.

I was part of a DUI team one Saturday night until going off duty at 3:00 a.m. the next morning. I had gotten to bed at 4:00 a.m. and returned two hours later for the 6:00 a.m. shift, when I headed out on patrol to check out the Blue Mountain recreation area. Our local Forest Service cops had asked me to do so, due to recent criminal activity in the area.

I was traveling on Route 365, a gravel road in which the bumps were just the ticket for a sleep-deprived trooper who needed to stay awake until his partner arrived for the 8 a.m. coffee break.

Driving up to the recreation area, I spotted something unusual in its entrance. One of the complaints I had heard concerned trash that had been dumped at the site. As I drew closer while scanning the ground for litter, I was shocked to see the body of a nude female lying on the road with her clothes stacked neatly beside her.

After calling dispatch to ask for the homicide unit to respond, my mind went on high alert as I approached the body to check for signs of life. I could see that her skin's bluish-purple state of lividity had already begun to set in as the blood pooled in her back, neck, and buttocks, indicating she had probably been deceased for a while. I was not surprised when I reached to check her pulse and found none. She was cool to the touch, with blue lips and glazed-over eyes.

What struck me the most was her familiar appearance. My daughter Kristi's best friend, Amber, had spent the night at our house. When I left for work that morning, I noticed Kristi's and Amber's granny boots by the door. For that reason I knew that the victim could not be Amber, despite the fact that the victim's hair color, approximate age, and physical size were comparable to Amber's. Nonetheless, a lump lodged in my throat at the sight of similar granny boots on the ground.

The victim's body lay posed in an apparently sexual position, which further raised my fear and stirred my ire. How could some bestial brute be so callous as to kill and then dump another human being on the cold ground in such a despicable way? I was livid at the thought. For this was someone's beloved daughter, and some unsuspecting parent was about to receive a visit that every parent dreads and prays will never happen.

As I retraced my steps and backed out of the crime scene, I waited for the sheriff's department to arrive to conduct an investigation.

The victim had worked at a local fast-food restaurant. The investigation uncovered the fact that her manager had been infatuated with her. It did not take long for the sheriff's department to build a case against the wretch. As it was, she had agreed to go out with him, and then at some point he forced himself upon her. He was rotund and she was tiny. His sheer weight had caused her to suffocate. How terrifying must have been those final moments for her.

It turned out that the apple did not fall far from the tree. The rapist's father as the suspect in a rape case had committed suicide on the same road years earlier. Junior followed in his father's footsteps, but lacked the will to do society a favor by taking his own life just as his father had taken his. With overwhelming forensic evidence of his wrongdoing, the court convicted Junior of his crime.

If there could be anything redeeming about this horrific tragedy, then most assuredly it would be nothing short of the saving grace of God, transforming what was thoroughly evil into something good that only God in his infinite wisdom and mercy could possibly bring about. In that regard, Saint Paul's words come to mind.

"I am persuaded, that neither death, nor life, nor angels, nor principalities, nor powers, nor things present, nor things to come, Nor height, nor depth, nor any other creature, shall be able to separate us from the love of God, which is in Christ Jesus our Lord" (Rom 8:38–39).

CHAPTER ELEVEN

The Golden Years: The Rookie Rides Again

I thoroughly enjoyed my time with the Montana Highway Patrol, yet I had aspirations of being promoted at some point. As I said earlier, we were tired of moving. Having decided that Missoula was to remain our home, I knew I would need to leave the highway patrol if I wished to be anything beyond a patrol officer.

By then, I had several friends on the Missoula County Sheriff's Department, including Carl Ibsen. If I were going to make one last career change, the time had come to do it. So I began the application process in 1996. During that preliminary period, which amounted to my last year with the highway patrol, I worked shifts with my partner Mike Burman whom I greatly enjoyed.

In August 1997, I was sworn in as a Missoula County deputy sheriff. For the first ten days I had the distinct honor of being both a Montana Highway patrolman and a Missoula County deputy as I burned off my excess leave-time from the former. I suppose it could be said that I was experiencing an identity crisis because I wasn't quite sure which badge and gun to carry when I was off duty.

I did not know that the day I was to be sworn in as a Missoula County deputy would be the beginning of the best years of my career. Nor did I know that those years would be my last as a regular officer. It was only fitting that Sheriff Doug Chase was the one to swear me in. He had been present years before when I was sworn in as a Missoula City officer.

As a career officer, my experience with the sheriff's department was more fun than anywhere else. Even though over the course of my career I had had the privilege of working with some of the greatest officers, the brotherhood of the sheriff's department stood above them all.

It certainly is true that all I had gone through in my previous departments had caused this wide-eye young rookie to mature into a seasoned officer. Nevertheless, I was required to undergo field training yet again before I could be released to work on my own. Although I was a known entity, which allowed for an abbreviated training period, I was not given a free pass by any stretch of the imagination.

Many officers tend to believe that a sheriff's department is harder to work for because of its politics. Granted, politics exist in every police organization, yet I genuinely felt that the sheriff's department afforded me more freedom to do my job than previous departments. While we were expected to maintain a high standard of properly executed work, we were also treated with respect. And since we knew what we were doing, there was little need for Monday-morning quarterbacking.

* * *

The truth is that an officer never knows what will transpire during a traffic stop. After pulling over a young lad whom we'll call Mr. Lord of the Rings, I discovered that he had some warrants outstanding for his arrest.

Mr. Lord of the Rings was an "illustrated" man, so to speak—in dress a throwback to the sixties, sporting a lip ring and ear rings. As I placed him under arrest, he commented, "Officer, please don't freak out on me!"

I had him secured in handcuffs as I stepped around his side and asked him if he was implying that he had a weapon or needles on him that I needed to be concerned about. "No, officer," he said; "It's, nothing like that. I just have nipple rings, and I figured you might want to know."

Sure enough, my search bore this out. At a time when skin piercings had not yet come into vogue, I suppose he was somewhat of a visionary. Either that, or he was aspiring to be an extra in the "Lord of the Rings" movie. Each to his own, I say, but the nipple is not a part of my body that I'd ever give consent to stick with a needle. It hurts just to think about it.

* * *

Domestic disturbances are commonplace in our profession. Usually they take care of themselves without needing to make an arrest. But when alcohol is involved I must refer back to my previous statement about God looking out for drunks and fools. Hence another example!

Dispatch sent me one night to a small apartment complex in Lolo to remove someone from the location. Upon arrival I spoke with the complainant and her boyfriend, who had been arguing with one another. The situation had not turned physical, so he agreed to leave of his own volition.

As often happened in such situations, I later received a call to return to the apartment because the boyfriend, Mr. Idiot, had also returned to the scene, and the two of them had gotten into a physical altercation causing the girlfriend to incur slight injuries.

She said that Mr. Idiot had run out of the apartment just before my arrival, and that he had grabbed a couple of cases of beer before taking off.

Checking the parking lot, I spotted him walking toward a carport with the beer cases in hand, at which point he spotted me and I ordered him to stop. However, he had other plans.

When he rounded the corner I rushed to the front and once again ordered him to stop. As he continued running past me, the load of beer cases slowed him down to the point that once I caught up with him he stumbled into a virtual sled-ride on top of the hoard of beer, and I landed on top of him like a rodeo cowboy wrestling a steer to the ground.

Once we came to a halt, I handcuffed him and turned him face-up, only to notice blood on my hands. I checked myself for injuries. Yet it was not I who bled. It was he. For beneath the cases of beer lay a butcher knife.

Needless to say, I was immensely grateful that Mr. Idiot had been more interested in escaping with his stash of beer than in skewering me, for which I thanked God and the beer for saving my life.

* * *

Carole and I were very active in our church and its youth group, as were our two older daughters. We knew all of their friends who forever were playing pranks on me although I always seemed to catch them in the act and ruin their fun.

One night while on break I stopped by a youth activity and stayed for dinner. When I later walked back to my patrol car, I found it not only toilet papered but also Saran wrapped. We all had a good laugh and then the kids removed their handiwork.

An hour or so later I discovered some underage adults drinking at the Blue Mountain Recreation area. They had begun to drink just before I got there, so I confiscated their beer before any of them had a chance to consume an excessive amount. Since they were most cooperative, I started to write up a summons for them to appear in court, just as one of them noticed remnants of toilet paper beneath my windshield wiper and quipped, "You have to be kidding! Someone actually toilet papered your car? Man, they really must hate you."

"No," I said. It was just the opposite. They did it because they love me."

The boy was shocked that anyone would like, much less love, a cop. I reminded him that we were human just as he was, and that we put our pants on one leg at a time. From then on, the conversation seemed to go well. I think he may have actually concluded that I was human after all.

* * *

On Fridays and Saturdays we often worked overtime on a Kegger patrol detail designed to curb traffic accidents and other incidents resulting from underage drinking. During one such shift, I received a tip about a house party in Lolo. When several other officers and I arrived, the kids quickly scattered. As they sought to race out the back door, I corralled several of them, gave them citations, and then waited for their parents to pick them up.

Upon learning that their son had been cited, one set of parents became very indignant, fearing that the citation would affect Junior's status on the football team. I told them that I had cited everyone at the party equally. The family fought the ticket at court and lost the case. But then guess who was the one I caught drinking at another party the following weekend—none other than Junior. Once again the family fought the ticket under the premise that I had picked on their poor child. I replied by saying that unfortunately he was lucky enough to be in the wrong place at the wrong time.

Subsequently, when I encountered Junior drinking a third time, the parents suddenly became concerned that he might have a drinking problem and would need help. In an effort to point them in the right direction, I encouraged them to get a hold of the county attorney. Regrettably, it was all too common for parents to be in denial about their child's behavior, which served only to reinforce the juvenile's acting out.

* * *

The school year had just begun when the sergeant from another shift called me one evening to ask that I come in on my day off to cover for an officer who was sick. During the course of the evening I stopped a speeding car full of teenage girls. While speaking with them, I noticed open containers of beer in their car. As they stepped out at my request, several bottles of wine and beer fell from the rear passenger floor board.

I cited all of them for illegal possession of alcohol, including the driver who had not been drinking. When the driver's parents arrived, they accused me of being totally unreasonable by citing their daughter. I explained that since she was knowingly driving with alcohol in the car, she was as responsible as the girls who were drinking. Although I commended her for being sober, I suspected that she simply hadn't yet taken the opportunity to imbibe. Her visibly upset father, a retired military officer, protested the citation, saying she was an excellent student. But I stood my ground and reaffirmed my decision to cite her. I wished them a better night and cleared the scene.

Fast forward to a Sunday night the following spring. The same sergeant once again had called me to work during my day off. I was located on the opposite side of Missoula where I stopped a vehicle for a suspected DUI. You can imagine my surprise at finding the same girl I had cited the previous fall, this time accompanied by an intoxicated male several years her senior. I arrested her for illegal possession of alcohol and a DUI. I arrested the adult man for contributing to the delinquency of a minor.

Her parents were quite distraught when they arrived at the station. They admitted that while their daughter had previously been an A student, in recent months she had been partying in addition to experiencing some other problems. As a consequence, they had moved her to an alternative school where she was failing most of her classes.

They asked me, "What can we do?"

I replied, "You don't recognize me, do you?" which they didn't.

I explained that I was the same officer who had arrested their daughter the previous fall. I further explained that this was not my regular shift, and that I was called upon to work this shift for only the second time in a year. After asking them what the odds were that I would be the arresting officer twice in the same year, I said, "I think someone is trying to tell you something."

I pointed them again to the county attorney's office for help, with the suggestion that they seek treatment for their daughter. This time they apologized for their daughter's actions.

Incidentally, I later arrested their adult son due to warrants outstanding for his failure to appear in court on criminal charges. The parents had pulled their hair out over him as well. I could not help but think that, had appropriate discipline been applied to the seat of learning when they were young kids, maybe things would have turned out differently. The parents weren't bad people but they had indulged their kids with every conceivable and unnecessary thing that their children could possibly want, which doubtlessly contributed to the kids' inability to manage their adolescent impulses.

Was it a coincidence that I happened to be the one to arrest their daughter in both instances? I think not. God has a way of steering us into the paths of others when we are most needed. As parents, we have a God-given responsibility to raise our children not only to be responsible individuals but for them to be responsive to God's will and purpose for their lives. "Train up a child in the way he should go: and when he is old, he will not depart from it" (Prov 22:6).

* * *

The last time I faced gunfire was in the wintertime when I was called to the scene of a domestic disturbance. As the other officers and I arrived, bullets flying from a trailer greeted us. Fortunately, no one was hit. We were confronted with what in police lingo is a "barricaded suspect incident."

After several hours of covering the perimeter while lying low in the snow and freezing off our hind ends, the SWAT team entered the residence only to discover that the suspect had used his earlier gunfire to shield his escape before we could surround the house. A day or so later he was arrested. Being on patrol is fraught with all kinds of danger and uncertainty, which is half of the job's fun. Officers never know what to expect.

While I was on Kegger patrol one evening, the dispatcher sent out a "be on the lookout" for a possibly suicidal person alleged to be armed, whose last direction of travel had been in my general vicinity. Patrolling the mountain road, I came upon a pull-off that trailed about thirty yards into the trees where I noticed a parked vehicle that matched the dispatcher's description.

I approached the vehicle expecting to see that the person had committed suicide. Peering in, I noticed that he lay on the seat, apparently having passed out with a pistol in his hand.

In order to remove him safely from his vehicle, I back-tracked to my patrol car and awaited the arrival of my backup who was thirty minutes away. Together, we quietly opened the car's unlocked doors and I quickly retrieved the weapon. After awakening the man we took him into custody and transported him to the hospital for voluntary commitment.

Unexpected eventualities and dreadful possibilities sometimes have happy endings.

* * *

Cops learn to follow their instincts. More often than not, things work out for the better. Partners learn to trust one another the longer they work together. When our supervisors knew that we had good instincts, they were more willing to step out on a limb for us.

Such was the case on a cold winter night. Several days prior the city police department had received a tip saying that a wanted fugitive was in town, having escaped from prison in Louisiana where he was serving a sentence for murder. The fugitive had discovered that his ex-wife lived in Missoula where he sought to see her. But family members tipped off the city police.

As the officers arrived at the house, the subject escaped out the back door. They lost him after undertaking a brief foot chase. The media then posted the fugitive's picture on the television news, describing him as armed and dangerous. Three nights later, I received a police report concerning a complaint that had come from the sister of the fugitive's wife. When I spoke with her she said that she had gotten a series of calls throughout the evening from a caller who said nothing to her and quickly hung up each time that she answered the phone. She suspected the fugitive had tried to reach his wife, believing her to be at her sister's house.

At first I thought the anonymous phone calls were a coincidence, and yet the more I thought about them, the more I believed that there was something to them. So I took the information to my supervisor and told him that my gut instinct said that the person could well be the fugitive. He agreed and we contacted the phone company to explain the situation.

Because of the serious threat the fugitive posed to the public so long as he remained at large, we were able to obtain the address from which the calls originated, which was an older home that had been converted to apartments.

Sergeant Reed, Deputy Tillman, and I went to the address, along with support from city police units. The apartment turned out to be that of a local drunk who possessed no phone. So we knocked on the door across the hallway where an intoxicated male answered.

Since the unit appeared to be a flop house, we asked the man if he was the renter. When he replied that he was, we showed him a picture of the fugitive whom he recognized. He said that the person had shown up a couple of days before, and that he had befriended him. Since then, the two had been partying.

We requested permission to search the premises, at which point the renter said he had been asleep prior to our arrival, and that during that time the suspect had left the apartment.

Deputy Tillman searched one room while I stepped into another room facing the street. Trash and bedding littered the floor. One pile in particular caught my attention, a stack of blankets with a sleeping bag beneath. As I looked closely, I noticed a slight movement.

I immediately ordered the person out at gunpoint and made it clear that I had better see his hands empty as he exited the sleeping bag. He slowly crawled out.

He was in fact the fugitive for whom we had been looking. After cuffing him, a check of his sleeping bag revealed a can of bear spray which I questioned him about. He admitted that he had planned to spray me with it until I let him know that I meant business.

Thankfully, I had trusted my instincts, which clearly paid off. Everyone including the fugitive left without getting hurt, which resulted in a good outcome to an anxious night.

As a footnote to the episode, my eldest daughter Kristi had ridden along with me in the patrol car that evening. Never in her wildest dreams had she ever thought she would accompany me as I transported a murderer and prison escapee. Not only did she learn just how dangerous our job in law enforcement could be, but she also gained a sense of peace in knowing that my fellow officers had my back.

About 1998, the Missoula County Deputy Sheriff's Association gave a great public relations tool to each officer—trading cards to hand out to kids in schools and neighborhoods. Over the years, I was amazed at how many adults wanted them, too. Each card contained an officer's picture and a safety message from the officer. As a result, I felt that the public saw us as a bit more human than before we passed out those cards. The cards also had a way of assuring the public that we were there to have their backs whenever perilous situations arose or dangerous persons threatened to do harm to law-abiding citizens.

* * *

The last year and a half prior to my retirement proved to be both fulfilling and trying. I had to admit that it took its toll on me physically and emotionally.

While traveling Highway 93 north toward Missoula for the shift briefing one afternoon, I noticed smoke rising above the approaching hill. I assumed that a house was on fire. Yet when I topped the hill, I came upon a head-on collision that had just occurred. Passers-by were stopping to see if they could help.

A full-sized van had smashed into a small pickup that had crossed the center line head-on into the van. Both vehicles were in flames. The pickup was already ablaze in the passenger compartment. With the assistance of bystanders I pulled out the driver. We patted out the flames on his clothing before making a medical assessment. He was not breathing.

An off-duty firefighter stopped to help. The two of us began administering CPR. Upon my first compression I realized that the victim had a flail chest. With all of his ribs and sternum broken, his rib cage offered no resistance and collapsed into his spine.

By this time, the fire had broken through the firewall of the other vehicle. So I left the first victim in the care of the firefighter and rushed to the van in which I found the driver unconscious. As flames licked at his feet, an emergency room physician on vacation assisted me with getting him to safety, and continued to attend him as I ran to the opposite side of the van to check for other victims.

As I reached for the sliding passenger door, and pulled it open, the gas tank ruptured. Flames immediately engulfed the van. Fortunately, the driver had been the lone occupant. Had there been others, then my efforts to save them would have been in vain.

It was later determined that driver of the pickup had been intoxicated at the time of the collision. He died of injuries from the impact. Due to our efforts, however, the driver of the van survived.

For my actions, the sheriff's department awarded me the sheriff's Star for Valor, yet the award was not mine alone. It belonged just as much, if not more so, to those who assisted me.

While I appreciated the recognition, my intrinsic reward consisted of being alive yet another day on the job that I loved.

* * *

Drunk drivers continued to be my priority due to the death and carnage that I had witnessed over the years as a result of their irresponsibility on the road.

While patrolling one time with a reserve deputy, we stopped a Jeep for a suspected DUI. The driver instantly became agitated and broke free from us as we sought to place him under arrest. He proceeded to grab an ax handle from the back of the Jeep and swung it at us as we tried to tackle him. It took not only the two of us, but also a second deputy backing us up, plus a rookie-in-training, to restrain the man and handcuff him. Only later did I realize that, some years prior, as a city police officer, I had arrested the same slow learner for a similar DUI.

On yet another stop, I asked a driver to exit his vehicle and undergo sobriety tests. The guy appeared at first glance to be wearing some type of apron. But he was actually dressed in a pair of white shorts turned inside-out.

Now and again, a patrol officer encounters the most bizarre of situations. For that man with his shorts turned inside-out had just come from the Testicle Festival at Rock Creek, which was an annual gala where people ingested cow testicles as they imbibed alcohol, lots and lots of alcohol.

Why were his shorts inside-out? Some questions are better left unanswered. The end result was that he received an all-expenses-paid overnight stay in the luxury accommodations of our county's gray bar hotel and resort.

* * *

Each year we received from the sheriff's department a discretionary allowance to update or replace our uniforms and equipment. During my last summer with the department, I used my allowance to purchase a patrol rifle since the department issued only shotguns. We were allowed to purchase our own patrol rifles, subject to policy restrictions that determined what types of rifles we could carry.

I had just qualified with my new rifle that week, when I set out to back up a fellow officer in Frenchtown. We were summoned to a residence where an armed person threatened to commit suicide.

And there we encountered an extremely intoxicated male with a shotgun.

Being short-handed, since other sheriff's units were busy elsewhere, we found ourselves strictly on our own. In order to contain the armed subject, I took one corner of the house and my partner took the other. Being in imminent danger due to my distance from the subject and his shotgun, I opted for my rifle.

I thought to myself, Oh, great! We may have to shoot this guy, and my new rifle will be tied up as evidence in court for who knows how long!

For sure, it was crazy to be more concerned about the rifle than the subject as a person, but the weirdest sorts of things go through one's mind when facing a loaded weapon.

We spent the next half hour trying to get the guy to put down his shotgun and surrender. After much pleading with him to drop it, he made a strange request. He asked if we would get him a beer.

We decided to roll with it.

We let him know that we would get him a beer, but only if he dropped the weapon. He agreed to do so as soon as he saw the beer.

I covered the suspect while my partner flanked him and moved toward the fellow's cooler on the opposite side of the house. Retrieving one of the beers from the cooler, my partner extended his hand around the corner of the house, holding the beer out to the suspect. True to his word, the suspect dropped the weapon and we took him into custody.

I transported the poor soul to the hospital. On the way, I persuaded him to agree to a voluntary commitment. Charges against him would have to await.

The moral of the story, if there is one, is that in order to effect a positive outcome in such a precarious circumstance, it's important to think on one's feet and to have every tool in the toolbox handy, including, if need be, a cooler stocked with beer.

* * *

Probably the most gut-wrenching moment a cop can experience is to receive an emergency call involving a person he knows, or a member of his own family.

My zone partners and I were on a break one Friday afternoon when we received a call to respond to a major accident on

Highway 93 south, just north of Lolo. The collision involved three vehicles. A medical life-flight helicopter was bound for the scene. We knew that it had to be a terrible wreck, so we headed out to assist the highway patrol with traffic control.

When we arrived on the scene, the highway was blocked in both directions. So we stationed officers to limit the possibility of additional accidents. Then we turned our attention to getting the life-flight landed safely and ready to transport.

A fellow officer advised me of a man fatally injured in one car. Life-flight was to transport his wife and infant daughter to the hospital. A person remained trapped in the vehicle that apparently caused the accident, and a third vehicle contained an unresponsive young girl.

Once the life-flight was in air, I finally had the opportunity to survey the entire scene. While doing so, another officer informed me that the deceased man and his wife and daughter were all related to a former partner at the Missoula City Police Department. The deceased man had been that partner's son. Without mentioning their names for the sake of the family's continuing need for privacy, the father of the threesome died instantly, which was merciful, considering the fact that his infant daughter was pronounced dead minutes later. Their injuries were horrific.

I had known my former partner's son from the time he was a boy attending my church. The one consolation I could offer my friend was that his son's death was instantaneous and that he had not suffered. While the injured wife survived, it was with the horrendous knowledge that she had lost her husband and their daughter.

Upon checking the third vehicle, my heart sank as I realized that it was my assistant pastor's daughter's car.

Amber Knusten, as I have said, was my oldest daughter Kristi's best friend. She lay behind the wheel, unresponsive. The entire front end of her vehicle had taken a crushing blow. I later learned from the trooper investigating the accident that, upon crossing the center line, the suspect's vehicle hit Amber head-on. Amber's car jettisoned sideways a total of eight feet after impact. As her car spun around, the suspect's vehicle passed her before also striking my former partner's family head-on. The impact to all three vehicles was massive. The speed limit was sixty-five miles per hour, which meant that the combined force of colliding at that speed from opposite directions was the equivalent of 130 miles per hour.

I remained with Amber until the EMS transported her to the hospital, and then drove her mother to the emergency room where I stayed with the family. Sadly, Amber did not make it. I can still hear Lori's and Chris's cries of grief as they realized that their oldest daughter was never to come home again in this world.

In the days ahead, they handled her death with grace, but the pain was palpable. Her death and those of the other family caused me to realize just how fragile life is for all of us. Amber was a sweet Christian girl and a joy to be around. She had spent many hours and nights in our home. We loved her dearly. Her death, the closest experience to losing one of my own, knocked the wind from my sails. She had left her Bible open on the kitchen table, turned to a passage on death. Having just finished her devotions before heading into town, she told her parents that she loved them.

I will always be thankful to my pastor, Tim Johnson, for riding with me when I returned to my first shift after the accident. His counsel and company were a blessing.

The driver who caused the wreck had worked for a local company. He had intentionally failed to care for his diabetes. The general consensus was that he had hoped to obtain retirement based upon his disability. If memory serves me correctly, he served a year in jail for having taken the lives of three people.

While the law is not always fair, in my estimation it is still the best legal system in the world.

* * *

More often than not we are darned if we do and darned if we don't. The last summer before I retired, the Hell's Angels motorcycle gang decided to hold one of its annual meetings in Missoula.

Unfortunately, the Rainbow people decided to visit Missoula that same week. So local agencies were tasked with keeping peace between two vastly different factions of society. The sheriff's department knew well in advance of the scheduled arrival of Hell's Angels, whose meetings had produced considerable violence in other cities, principally because their municipal agencies were not well prepared.

At the time, Missoula did not realize just how stellar its law enforcement leadership was, vowing to maintain the peace. Under mutual aid agreements, extra officers as well as air assets from other departments in Montana and several western states were on hand to greet the Angels' arrival. Our leadership met with their leadership to make clear that the Angels were welcome, provided they behaved themselves. No violence would be tolerated.

Multiple shootings, stabbings, and murders had occurred in previous locations where the Angels had met. Our leadership vowed that this wouldn't happen in our city by going to great lengths to train our officers about gang criminal practices in order to ensure that we were prepared.

Unfortunately, some people in our community believed that we were treating the matter as if we were presiding over a police state. Yet most citizens, including the more liberal ones, had no idea of the bullet we were about to dodge due to the special training and increased police presence.

Missoula was fast becoming the Berkley of Montana, which this event was about to prove true. Local publicity spread to regional publicity. Before long, people were coming from other cities to protest what they viewed as law enforcement's overkill. The majority of demonstrators whom we later faced were not locals but professional out-of-state protesters.

After the first night, leadership from the Angels and our various departments spoke with one another. The Angels made it clear that they wanted to be left alone by an inquisitive public, but that the protesters were stirring matters up. They made it clear that, if we did not take care of the situation, then they would do so themselves.

Our efforts to protect the public resulted in a full-scale protest that required use of tear gas and the arrest of several people for disorderly conduct. What the protesters failed to understand was that we were trying to avoid the senseless shootings and murders that typically followed Hell's Angels' gatherings. Of all the arrests made that weekend, my recollection is that only one Angel was arrested on a nonviolent charge. A few more were cited for traffic violations.

The professional protesters and the media blew the entire episode out of proportion, giving our agencies a black eye. The several law-suits filed against us smeared our reputations. Nevertheless, we all did the best we could and were proud of the fact that no one was killed that weekend. Many in the community understood what we sought to do, but as is often the case, liberal media and professional protesters drowned out our voices.

* * *

During my last year in Missoula, I began to experience increased back pain, which I had first noticed when I was with the highway patrol. My left leg gave out on occasion, and I feared that eventually a citizen or fellow officer might get hurt, should I go down during a call because of my weakened leg. I knew I could not live with that scenario.

I went to a new physician who ordered a second MRI to compare with the earlier one taken five years before at the time of the injury. The diagnosis indicated an annular tear in my disk, present in both MRIs. Yet in that period of time it had become much worse.

Surgery in October 2000 resulted in my need to retire from the sheriff's department. The damage to my back, plus the botched first surgery, left me in far too much pain and a lack of mobility to continue working. I was devastated.

However, I figured that if I had to leave, then I might as well leave while at the top of my game. As I have said, my years with the Missoula County Sheriff's Department were the best of my career, for which I will always be immensely thankful.

CHAPTER TWELVE

The Rookie Rides Off into the Sunset, or Does He?

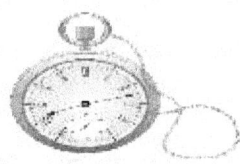

When I retired in March 2001, I believed that my life as a cop was over. But as I have often discovered, God apparently has a good sense of humor. Roughly two years before I retired, Carole asked if I would ever consider moving to Tennessee or Kentucky. I assured her that it was the furthest thing from my mind. After all, I had a career and no intention of leaving it. She asked if she could pray about it. I said that she could pray, which didn't mean that I was going to move. "Remember," I said, "I took the job at the sheriff's department because I didn't want to move anymore. Right?"

There is, however, that old expression, "Never say never."

When I knew that I must retire, I began to consider my options. I was very much involved in the life of Florence Baptist Church and felt that I was even called to preach. Once I retired there would be nothing to hold me back from doing so.

Staying in Montana was not an option, however, because we could not afford to live there on the small retirement income that I was due to receive. So, despite my intention never to move again, and much to my chagrin, we moved to Powell, Tennessee.

There I enrolled in classes at Crown College of the Bible. But within weeks I realized that I was not called to be a pastor. Once I had spent some time around men who were clearly called to preach, I realized it wasn't for me. They were consumed by preaching. While I enjoyed it, I was not consumed.

Being unwilling to quit what I had begun, I chose to pursue a path in youth ministry. I had always loved kids, so I figured that down the road I could help out with some type of youth ministry. I didn't have to work during my first year of school, so I concentrated on my studies.

When the tragedy of September 11, 2001, struck, I stood in shock with most of the country. We watched the events unfold on television monitors in the school's auditorium. Never had I wished to be in uniform again so much as I did that day. Had it not been for the condition of my back, I most assuredly would have reenlisted in the military or sought out a new law enforcement position. One minute I had been enjoying a beautiful September day while sitting on a park bench, and the next minute I watched people jumping out of windows to their deaths.

As I observed the towers collapse, I knew instinctively that not only civilian lives were lost, but also the lives of many firefighters and cops who were trained to rush into the thick of danger. My heart ached for the many who died, especially my brothers and sisters in blue and their families. Looking back on that day, it amazes me how quickly we as a nation have since forgotten the pain, the suffering, and the sacrifices of those people.

* * *

During my first summer at Crown College, Carole and Kristi were working at the Cedar Springs weekday school in Knoxville. Carole called me one afternoon to see if I would be interested in subbing. I submitted my application, and then for the next ten years I worked there, first part-time and eventually full-time. I became affectionately known as a real pre-Kindergarten cop, as opposed to the fictional Kindergarten one starring Arnold Schwarzenegger in the movie "Kindergarten Cop." Arnold had nothing on me, for I'm pretty sure I was better looking, as I reminded myself every day while preparing to go to work, singing the Mac Davis song, "Oh Lord, It's Hard to Be Humble." Hey, A guy can dream, you know!

* * *

Working with the kids, this old cop pretty much lost all of his dignity. If my former law enforcement partners had seen half of what I did, I suspect they would have revoked my "man-card."

One incident from that era is worth sharing for the good laugh it presents at my expense. At the time, Carole and I were working together in a classroom. It was pajama day for the kids, and the teachers were expected to dress up as well. My own children have made a habit of buying me silly pajamas over the years, so on this occasion I wore my Super Man pajamas. The kids loved it, so I figured I could roll with it.

Usually on pajama day I would change into street clothes before going home. Heaven forbid that I should be seen in public wearing my pajamas. But on this particular day I was bone tired. So I suggested that Carole drive us home. I cautioned her not to make any stops along the way. We were on the main road leading to our home, with about four minutes to go, when suddenly we came upon a rollover accident having just occurred.

I had been napping in the car. So when we pulled up to the accident, I awoke and sprang into action. I jumped out through the passenger door and ran toward the victim who was crawling out from his car while simultaneously speaking with his daughter on his cellphone. His face was bloody, but otherwise he appeared in relatively good shape considering what had just happened to him.

As I drew closer to him, his eyes widened as he looked at me. He then turned back to his phone and promptly told his daughter that everything was okay because, he said, "Superman is here!"

I stopped in my tracks and for the first time took stock of what I was wearing and assured him that indeed I was not Superman, but I was a retired police officer there to help.

My mind was foggy, so I missed a great opportunity to let him know that I had stayed the previous night in a Holiday Inn Express. I hate it whenever I miss a chance to be witty, but nevertheless I wisely donned my jacket before the active-duty police arrived, lest they haul me off to the funny farm.

* * *

By the time 2004 rolled around I was mostly using a cane to get around. Things were heading downhill quickly. Fortunately, my pastor, Clarence Sexton, told me about a surgeon at the Norton Weatherman Spine Institute in Louisville, Kentucky. His name was Dr. Mitch Campbell, one of the top orthopedic surgeons in the country.

Dr. Campbell operated on me in February 2004. It took several months of rehab and recovery, but in the end I felt like a new man. I can't thank Pastor Sexton enough for sending me to Dr. Campbell because he gave me a new lease on life. I wasn't sure that I could take the rough and tumble of the street again, but my condition had drastically improved. I learned a valuable lesson with

Dr. Campbell. There are physicians who are A-students and some who are C-students. Dr. Campbell trained and took his residency at the same schools as my first surgeon, who shall remain nameless. But my first surgeon was nowhere near the caliber of Dr. Campbell.

I sought to find several other jobs but the job service kept directing me towards law enforcement and security. I even heard that the Marines were looking for a few good men. But I ruled out the Marines and full-time law enforcement because I figured that, due to my spinal medical history, I could never pass the physical exam. Not that it mattered, because I am fairly certain that Carole would have broken both of my legs before I ever enlisted. She said something to the effect that she was finally getting used to me and that it would be way too hard to train a new husband.

* * *

At the end of 2004, I was approached by a church member and friend, Daryl Johnson, who asked if I would consider helping him set up Crown College's security department. Over the next few months we gave birth to that department, which is still standing today to protect the school and its students. We were not large enough to become our own police department, but the county sheriff deputized us as special deputies with powers to arrest, which we hoped we would never need. I worked there for the next three years. I left because I realized that the night shift was the only one I'd ever get to work. I guess I had mellowed since the days when the night shift was my favorite, but I no longer wanted to be a nocturnal creature.

I went to work for the St. Mary's hospital system in July 2007. By then, we had moved as a family to Sevierville, Tennessee, which in its more rural setting reminded me at times of Missoula. I continued to work part-time for the Cedar Springs weekday school and for Crown College, then later for St. Mary's where I was also deputized. For a while I was back to shift work with its incentive to receive considerably more pay. I spent the vast majority of my time at St. Mary's in the emergency room, dealing with psychiatric, intoxicated, and drug-abuse patients.

One day, I was watching over a series of rooms when I was called away for a few minutes to the emergency room to assist with a violent person who had overdosed in an attempt to commit suicide. Once the patient was safely in restraints for her protection I returned to the rooms I had been monitoring.

Once I arrived, a patient, who earlier had been restrained, walked out of his room after slipping out of his restraints. He seemed amiable enough while a nurse and I talked him into going back to his room. But that quickly changed when I told him he would have to be placed back in his restraints. Being a little guy whom I referred to as Shorty, he must have fancied himself to be a boxer, for he took a swing at me. As I ducked his punch, I sought to kick the gurney out of the way as I had done so many times before in order to gain control of the patient. Unfortunately for me, all of the gurneys had just been replaced with pedestal beds for a softer and gentler approach to treatment. As you might guess, there is not a lot of give to a pedestal bed. So I buckled my knee against it, which caused me to drop to the floor on my other knee. Shorty then took the opportunity to leap on my back and put me in a choke hold, which made me appear as though I was giving him a piggyback ride.

I rose to my feet and tried to dislodge him by bouncing him off of all four walls. For a little guy, he was as strong as the Pillsbury Dough Boy on angel dust. And, believe me, that is strong!

In that moment, all of my previous training kicked in. But Shorty was quite determined to make good on his escape, because he clung to me for all he was worth until I finally grayed out and collapsed to the floor.

Thankfully, Shorty simply wanted to get away without hurting anyone, so he did not go for my weapon. As I returned to consciousness, I grabbed the first thing I could get my hands on, which was his gown. With that, Shorty took off like a bullet from a gun. His plump, naked body rippled as he ran out a side door of the ER and through the operating suites before coming back through the ER again.

Shorty's brief escape ended abruptly when he attempted to run through a locked door. There my partners ended the game of Keystone Cops by taking the dazed renegade back into custody. In addition to his other offenses, Shorty was charged and later convicted of assaulting an officer.

* * *

In 2010, the hospital changed hands. Fortunately, when it soon became apparent that its new management was not for the better, Cedar Springs offered me a full-time teaching position that enabled me to leave the hospital before it all fell apart. Carole and I taught together for the first year, with me as her assistant. She moved on to take care of the nursery the next year as I became the lead teacher of the K-four-and-five pre-Kindergarten class. I had a blast teaching the little ones. Yet for the next two years I was sicker than I had ever been because anything they caught, I caught.

In 2011, I had my right knee replaced. Thirty-three years of bone-on-bone finally had destroyed the joint. So I sported chrome in my knee and titanium in my back, imagining that sometime in the past the chrome must have come from a 1957 Chevrolet bumper, and the titanium from an M-1 Abrahams tank. What an awesome combination, I thought. I recalled the "Six Million Dollar Man" movie series from the 1970s, figuring that I was well on the way to becoming the bionic Steve Austin, one implant at a time.

By this time, being sick had become the norm. I knew I would need to get away from all of the little people if I expected to get any better.

I was shopping in Walmart one day when I came across Todd Beeler, a former church member and police officer. By then Todd was working as a school security and resource officer for the Knox County School District in Knoxville, Tennessee. He encouraged me to apply. I told him that while it was appealing, I did not think the district would hire me, given my back and knee issues. He assured me that the department was specifically looking for retired cops, and that as long as I could get through their nine-week training academy, then I would be okay. I went home that night and discussed it with Carole. Then after considering it for several more days I applied.

* * *

The month of August 2015 found me at the age of fifty-six attending the fifth training academy of my career. There were many days when I questioned why I was doing this to myself again. I was the grandpa of the class and was regularly reminded of it. I passed the academy training and in November and went to work at an inner city high school.

To say that I was in for some culture shock was a gross understatement. Appalled was the right word. The gang culture permeated the school. It manifested itself in constant fights and shoving contests. My impression was that while the students demanded one another's respect, no matter how wrong they were, that respect was not afforded anyone else among school administrators, teachers, staff, or officers. It did not take me long to realize that the apple frequently fell not far from the tree as I watched parents dropping off their kids morning after morning, long after the bell had rung. The absentee and tardiness rates were unacceptable.

The school had some excellent teachers and administrators who did their absolute best under less than optimal conditions. They cared about the kids and truly tried to give them a quality education. The school had so much to offer, yet so many refused to seize the opportunity right in front of them. It clearly took the right kind of adult to work in such an environment.

I knew by the end of the school year that I was not that person. I don't pretend to understand all of the socioeconomic factors that pertained to the situation. But I found it especially difficult to understand the students whose immediate goal in life was to become a drug dealer or give birth to as many kids as possible in order to receive government subsidy. It seemed that the lack of positive familial goals and reinforcements, as well as the exploitation of government programs, served only to render the kids incapable of achieving anything above the lowest of expectations. And that saddened me.

High school should be about becoming a responsible adult and developing aptitudes and skills for living a meaningful and purposeful life. Socially, inviting a morally healthy date to the prom should be more important than hooking up with a malicious gang, only to be beaten or shot down. Most if not all of the kids could have had a rewarding life if only they had accepted the positive influences the school offered them. Unfortunately, imitating the gang culture of the hood too often prevented it from happening.

I thought at first that if parents were to see what truly went on in the school, they would be shocked. But then I met some of the parents and witnessed their interactions. Not only were they not shocked by what transpired among the kids, but by their own poor examples they modeled many of the same behaviors. Since when did rudeness, vulgarity, tardiness, and incorrigible conduct become okay in school? As a society, we are losing an entire generation of kids due to seriously flawed parenting.

Discrimination in any form is wrong. Yet, by the end of the school year, I came to understand the nature of reverse discrimination. In many instances, I was held in contempt by virtue of the color of my skin and the uniform I wore. I couldn't trust even the kids with whom I felt I had made significant inroads. I thought that if I should ever go down in a fight, they would put their boots to me because of the collective mentality and conformity of the gang culture. It wouldn't matter whether they liked me or not. They feared punishment by their fellow gang members if they showed any affinity for the police.

I knew that at my age it was not a matter of whether I might be injured, but rather of when and how badly. The environment was more conducive to a young buck than it was to me.

I shared my concerns with the school division chief and he agreed. If there were ever a case of the inmates running the asylum, I had seen it. School administrators were unable to manage unruly student behavior, not because they lacked the desire to do so, but because their hands were tied when it came to enforcing appropriate disciplinary measures.

* * *

That year, I had two great partners from the Knoxville Police Department. The first was Officer Ricky Gallagher, who was injured along with two other Knoxville police officers while dealing with a student who could have been a football line-backer had he not been high on drugs.

I had been called to a classroom to escort the young man to the office. Yet it was apparent that the student was not going to go peaceably. I asked the teacher to clear the classroom in order to remove the audience which the student apparently wanted. Then I called for backup from Officer Gallagher.

My hope was that the student would be more apt to cooperate with two officers than with one. But I was wrong. As Officer Gallagher entered the classroom, the student took a healthy swipe at me. I ducked his swing and then imposed an arm bar takedown in an effort to wrestle him to the floor and safely restrain him. Officer Gallagher joined the struggle. Together we wrestled with the kid for the next five minutes until Officer Gallagher radioed for additional backup. Within a few minutes two more police officers arrived.

When dealing with a juvenile, the school required taking every precaution in order not to injure the student. For all of our combined efforts, none of us left unscathed. Ricky re-injured a knee. Another officer broke some ribs. Still another broke a finger. I sustained some bumps and bruises but was not seriously injured. The student was arrested for assaulting a police officer and resisting arrest.

My second partner, Officer Adam Wilson, replaced Officer Gallagher. He and I also became good friends as we worked together at the school to which I was next assigned. Adam was a top-notch officer who, like me, had great passion for the job as well as compassion for people. He assisted me in sponsoring the school's honor guard. We both were Christians, which was yet another thing we held in common. We had each other's backs and could always depend upon one another. One can't ask for more in a partner.

* * *

The following year I was transferred to Career Magnet, a public school open to students throughout the county, offering a specialized core curriculum in addition to basic studies. Students applied to attend and commonly were required to demonstrate from past records that they were capable of maintaining at least average grades. Throughout their high school years they took English, math, and other core courses. During their junior and senior years they could elect to take college-level classes and acquire college credit or obtain an associate's degree if they applied themselves.

Contrary to the school that I had left, the majority of kids at Career Magnet wanted to be there, which was a refreshing change. There I found a home and my niche as a resource officer. The student body consisted of an eclectic bunch of kids representing all races, religions, and socioeconomic backgrounds. Amazingly, it was more like a family than a school, though admittedly a much smaller school. The environment worked in the kids' favor because it fostered close relationships among students, and between students and faculty. While we were not without occasional problems, the small percentage of students who didn't want to be there were the ones who presented the most issues. That being said, we didn't experience nearly as many troublesome situations as the larger schools.

During the next two and a half years I became a counselor, an advisor, a confidant, and a friendly face, all while maintaining my posture as an officer. The kids knew that I would enforce the law if their behaviors necessitated it. Yet they understood that I would treat them fairly. They also knew that even when they messed up on occasion, as they did, I would not throw the baby out with the bath water.

The Lord God had forgiven my sins as far as the East is from the West. It was incumbent upon me to do no less with respect to the students.

For the most part, my days were filled with laughter. I grew up in a family in which teasing was customary and comprised a big part of me. With respect to my fun-loving and humorous side, the kids knew that I was an equal-opportunity wisecracker from whose jest and banter none of them were safe.

When I took the job, I realized that school resource officers were on the cusp of transforming public attitudes toward law enforcement. This was especially true at a time when the media critiqued our every move for the sake of a percentage of the population that wished to believe the worst about us. As in every profession, law enforcement had some bad actors. Yet it seemed to me that few professions were scrutinized to the extent that we cops were.

* * *

My primary function as a school resource officer was to form the first line of defense in the event that an active shooter ever darkened the door. Our responsibility was to create a safe and secure learning environment for students, staff, and administrators. We were to promote the best possible atmosphere in support of student success, which meant that I and my police department counterparts were responsible for dealing with enforcement, should things get out of hand.

I teased the kids daily about being scalawags, rascals, and never-do-wells, but they knew that they were *my* scalawags, *my* rascals, and *my* never-do-wells. They knew me as a person, not merely as a uniform to be feared. Above all, they knew that I would lay down my life for them if necessary. By presenting them with a positive presence, I hoped and prayed that they would look to law enforcement when needed, and respect law enforcement when necessary—the latter especially when they were on the receiving end of a ticket, or worse.

My office door was a revolving door. Students came to me with relationship, family, and school problems. They sought a shoulder to cry on, and at times a shoulder to punch. I encouraged kids in need of anger management to seek me out when they were feeling angry. If they needed something other than a student or wall to strike, then my shoulder patch was fair game. For those who deemed the idea a bit unorthodox, I made it clear that they could take aim only at the shoulder patch. While many came simply to vent, hoping I would calm them down, none ever took me up on my offer to be a surrogate punching bag.

During my first year at Career Magnet a kid sought me out in the hall one morning. It was clear that he was high on something. He said that he had a problem, that he had taken some drugs, and that he was feeling very sick and scared. What amazed me was that, of all the people in the school whom he could have approached, he chose to come to me. He did so, knowing that he would likely face a long suspension. Yet he trusted me, believing I would help him. Why? Because I had already dealt with him regarding some other issues, and he knew I would be fair. I say this, not to blow my own horn, but rather to emphasize that law enforcement's best community relations tool consists of building relationships with the people we serve.

Other kids approached me, not only about personal matters but also out of concern for the welfare of the school. They knew that if they told me something in confidence, I would not betray them. On one such occasion a student confided that some fellow students were doing drugs on campus. When I confronted them about it, they admitted as much and faced their punishment knowing that when they returned to school I would treat them no differently than I had before they made their error of judgment. They understood that they had broken their trust and must rebuild it, but I wasn't going to crucify them for it. If we are honest with ourselves, many of us did not make our best decisions either when we were in high school.

* * *

There were two things I learned from counseling my students. On the one hand, I discovered that many of them faced highly unfavorable circumstances at home and yet persevered in bettering themselves. On the other hand, many came from loving and supportive environments in which their parents actively engaged in their children's learning, setting positive examples for them by word and deed. Yet some of the latter kids complained whenever their parents applied appropriate discipline. I assured them that they would better understand someday when they became parents themselves.

Given a conducive learning environment at home or at school, good things are possible.

Case in point was that a number of the students at the Career Magnet school lived in that same gang-ridden neighborhood where the inner-city school was located. Yet because of the positive environment at Career Magnet, they dropped the gang mentality altogether and thrived.

As I attended our Career Magnet graduations, I was touched by the many students who sought me out to thank me. Thank me, I thought, for what? I was simply doing my job the best I knew how. Yet thank me they did. In as much as everyone is an example to someone else, either for good or ill, I thank God that he used me for some goodness with those kids.

While at work I wasn't permitted to proselytize, and rightfully so. I was paid a wage to be a resource officer, not an evangelist. That being said, I had many opportunities to share my faith as kids came to me with their problems. I didn't preach to them, but rather shared with them what God had done for me in similar circumstances. I liked to think that they thanked me out of personal respect. But, more importantly, I prayed that in the future they would respect the blue uniform for what it represents, and for the quality of people who represent it when they wear it.

* * *

Public school graduations were held throughout the week at the local university. My final graduation day began at 8:30 a.m. Yet that day's first graduation ceremony didn't take place until 1:00 p.m. When the last ceremony of the day was over at 10:30 p.m., I was more than ready to go home.

I don't know why I had noticed him, but earlier in the evening an older gentleman had passed through the gate that I was working at the graduation ceremony. Then, about an hour before the event ended, he left through the same gate. He was quite tall, wearing a white shirt and jeans, and carrying a long umbrella.

Just as we were about to clear the arena, a young lady approached me and told me that she was concerned about an older gentleman who appeared to have been abandoned in the parking lot. When she described him, I knew instantly the person she meant. I accompanied her for about two blocks before we found the gentleman.

It turned out that he was ninety-two years old and had come for his great grandson's graduation. His wife, also elderly, had waited in the car since she was not able to walk the distance to the ceremony. But then apparently she forgot him and drove home.

As I spoke with the gentleman I learned that he was a World War II veteran Marine. He had served in the South Pacific at the battle for Okinawa as a flame-thrower operator with the Sixth Marines. He spoke of the time that he was notified of President Roosevelt's death and how much he had mourned his loss.

He also mentioned the shock that he and others had experienced during their training to invade the Japanese homeland, when suddenly the atomic bomb was dropped to save American lives. He bore no ill will toward the Japanese, but he understood that others might.

Lastly, he spoke of spending eleven months in China during the Japanese occupation force's repatriation to Japan.

Like many of his generation, he returned home and attended college. He then went to work for the Tennessee Valley Authority in order to support his family. After devoting thirty years to the TVA he retired and became a farmer.

I knew through my own knowledge of combat history that the gentleman had been fortunate to survive such a mission on Okinawa. The mortality rate for flamethrower operators was very high. Having the good fortune over the course of that hour to speak with a living and breathing veteran of American history, I utterly forgot any lingering physical pain that I had from standing on my feet throughout the long workday.

When his great grandsons arrived to greet us, I was even more impressed to see what an honor and privilege they considered it to be to have him as their great grandfather, as they expressed appreciation for his service to the nation.

I was thankful to God for my being in the right place at the right time to meet the gentleman. And, should either of his great grandsons ever read these pages, they will know what an honor it was for me to assist their great grandfather, Richard Dottul.

* * *

In the latter months of my career, I developed more problems with my back, hips, and knees. Most older cops can relate to such things. The physical requirements of the job wear and tear on the body. Once again I was faced with not being able to perform at the top of my game. Because I wasn't willing to risk the safety of my school and my partners, after nearly three decades of service I determined that it was time to hang up my vest and gun belt.

I have been retired now for three years and am blessed still to be in contact with a number of the students I served at Career Magnet. It has been an honor and privilege to see several of them enter the military and serve their country. Others are occupied with various vocations, and some are raising a few scalawags of their own. Two have moved on to become officers, one with a neighboring county's sheriff's office and the other with a local police department. Yet still another is pursuing his dream of making a good living as a cowboy. I can't help but think of my lifelong friend, Mark Rosenbaum, who as a kid, just like me, wanted to pursue his dream and did so. I trust that the generation which I helped to mold will be as happy and fulfilled as he and I are.

* * *

Two years after I retired, Officer Adam Wilson was shot. He and three other officers were taking a youth into custody for an act of domestic abuse that occurred earlier in the day at the inner city school where Officer Wilson and I had met.

Packing a Glock pistol, the juvenile fired at the officers as they approached him in one of the school's restrooms, barely missing one of the officers.

One of Officer Adam's partners inadvertently shot Adam while aiming to hit the suspect who lay on the floor while the group of officers sought to disarm and handcuff him. The suspect was turning as if to fire on Adam when the shot that injured Adam was fired by his partner. Tragically, Adam had moved his leg in front of his partner's weapon just as he fired it. Such is the chaos that accompanies a close-quartered gunfight.

The juvenile male suspect tragically lost his life. Many in the community near the school blamed the police for his death. Instead of immediately assigning blame, it would have been better had they examined the situation closely by asking some basic questions.

Why had the kid carried a gun to school? Apparently, he did not have the gun on him when the school authorities called him to the office for questioning about the earlier assault.

Why did the kid not remain in the school office until a family member was found to come and get him? It was due to the fact that he refused, and also because the school lacked the authority to retain him there. Instead, he wandered the halls and then left the school and returned with his gun. Clearly, had he not possessed the gun, he would not have lost his life.

Why did he not comply with the police when they told him he was under arrest? Instead, he resisted arrest and fired at the officers. He failed to comply with their request because of the aggressive practices he had learned from the gang culture to which he belonged. Many of the parents of the gang members had been gang members themselves.

Why was he one of five teens from that school who were killed that same year in their own community? The other four were not victims of police shootings, but gang shootings. They were products of a neighborhood that thrived on gang violence, criminal activity, and drug usage.

Why as parents did they not raise their children to respect themselves, the property of others, and the lives of people with any skin color?

Why had the school system become so disempowered as to lack the authority to protect its students and faculty by disciplining thoroughly unacceptable behavior on the part of miscreants? In Knox County, a child could receive only so many suspensions before being readmitted. Suspension is too often not a sufficient deterrence. The vast majority of the kids seem not even to want to be in school to begin with.

If I sound angry, it's because I am. I am angry about a generation of kids dying needlessly because of the twisted culture they live in. I am angry that my friend was shot and likely will have a residual disability for the remainder of his life. I am angry because my brothers and sisters in the profession are slaughtered in streets all across the nation by people who have little or no respect for human life.

Finally, I am angry because segments of society, and society as a whole, instead of addressing root problems, remain unwilling to acknowledge the unhealthy dynamics that prevail within local communities as well as within the broader culture. In that sense, we all bear some degree of responsibility.

There are respectable people, from every race and creed within neighborhoods and communities, who lead by example and with foresight every day. At the same time, many seek to escape their poverty-ridden and crime-ridden environs to forge new and improved lives elsewhere, for themselves and their children.

What hope then is there for all of us? To what extent are we in this human enterprise together?

I take comfort in the fact that this was God's world long before it became ours, and it will remain God's world. For God is ever present within it.

I make no claim as to specifically how we must proceed, given the many problems that affect us in small and large measure. But I do claim that God has not abandoned us to ourselves. For surely God continues to open the way to the future, just has God has shown us the way through the past.

In that spirit, I conclude by reiterating what I said at the outset.

My life as a Christian has been nothing special, for it mirrors the lives of most Christians I know, each one of whom has experienced miracles.

I continue, as they, to live in the hope and expectancy of witnessing more miracles myself, every single day.

CHAPTER THIRTEEN

Remembering the Fallen: Gone, Yet Not Forgotten

In Honor There Is Hope

Throughout my career I have known six officers whose names now grace the solemn commemorative wall of the National Law Enforcement Officers Memorial in Washington, DC, at Judiciary Square. The stone memorial features two male and two female bronze lions, each watching over a pair of lion cubs. Raymond Kaskey sculpted the adult lions and George Call the cubs. A quotation appears beneath each of the lions.

"It is not how these officers died that made them heroes, it is how they lived." – Vivian Eney Cross, Survivor

"In valor there is hope." – Tacitus

"The wicked flee when no man pursueth: but the righteous are as bold as a lion." – Proverbs 28:1

"Carved on these walls is the story of America, of a continuing quest to preserve both democracy and decency, and to protect a national treasure that we call the American dream." – President George H. W. Bush[2]

    I was fortunate to have attended the memorial wall's dedication and later its ceremonial opening to the public. Although a time or two I came close having my name engraved upon it, I am thankful that I was alive to visit the memorial myself. Yet had I fallen in the line of duty, most certainly my name would have kept good company.

---

[2] "National Law Enforcement Officers Memorial Wall," Wikipedia, the Free Encyclopedia, last edited Jul 8, 2022, 09:18, https://en.wikipedia.org/wiki/National_Law_Enforcement_Officers_Memorial.

Throughout my career I attended a number of police funerals. At one time or another I worked with and knew six officers who gave their lives in full devotion to their duty, to their country, their profession, and the communities they served. I now share brief synopses of their stories and my relationship to them, in the sequence of their dates of death.

* * *

Ofc. Stephen A Lepaine of the Missoula City Police Department was killed on November 5, 1982, at approximately 2:00 a.m., when his patrol car was broadsided by a drunk driver traveling at a high rate of speed as he blew past a stop sign and struck Steve. Steve had been backing up another officer during a traffic stop. Even though Steve was wearing a seat belt, the impact was so violent that Steve ejected from his patrol car and struck a vehicle on the front line of a local car dealership. Another officer, a friend of mine, observed the accident from his rear-view mirror and to this day remains haunted by the memory. Steve left behind a wife, two sons, and three siblings. Cliff LePaine, one of his siblings, is a Missoula City officer. I had met Steve while I was an intern at the department. He had served the citizens of Missoula for three years at the time he was killed. The drunk driver was charged with vehicular homicide and convicted.

Ofc. Stephen A Lepaine 11/5/1982

* * *

Sgt. Allen Leslie Kimery
12/06/1984

Sergeant Allen Leslie Kimery of the Missoula County Sheriff's Department in Missoula, Montana, was gunned down on, December 6, 1984, during the traffic stop of a person who had run off from a service station with five dollars' worth of stolen gas. Unbeknown to Al, the suspect drove a stolen car from which he shot Al in the chest with a .357 magnum. Al returned fire and wounded the suspect, leaving sufficient evidence that led to the capture and ultimate conviction of his killer who received a sentence of twenty years to life in the Montana State Penitentiary where he was eventually killed by a fellow prisoner. This was small consolation to Al's wife Jo and his son and daughter.

Al had served the citizens of Missoula County for nine years prior to his death. I recounted my relationship to Al in chapters six and seven. As an aside, Al was in large part responsible for the issuing of body armor to both Missoula City and Missoula County. He was killed just a few blocks from where I was shot three years later. The fatal wound to his chest was located in approximately the same spot as my nearly fatal wound. Because I survived and he did not, the two departments saw the wisdom of purchasing body armor vests for their officers.

* * *

Sergeant John Conner III of the Manassas Police Department in Manassas, Virginia, was shot and killed on July 24, 1988, in an ambush-style attack when responding to the report of a suspect who earlier had been involved in a domestic disturbance and was sitting on his front porch, firing a rifle. John was approaching the residence from the rear of the property when, due to the arrival of other police units, the suspect moved to the back of the house. Unbeknown to John, a motion light mounted on the eave made John an easy target. John and the suspect exchanged shots. The suspect was wounded in the foot. John was shot three times with a fatal wound to the back of his head.

Sgt. John Conner III
07/24/1988

John had been our military police traffic sergeant when I was stationed at Fort Belvoir. He joined the Manassas Police Department a year before I joined the Prince William County Police Department in the same county. He had served the citizens of Manassas for eight years before being slain. He left behind his wife and four children. The suspect was convicted of murder and executed nine years later.* * *

Corporal Charles William Hill of the Alexandria City Police Department in Alexandria, Virginia, was shot to death March 22, 1999. As a member of the Alexandria SWAT team, Corporal Hill was called one day to a hostage situation. A drug dealer from New York City, who had come to Virginia to collect a drug debt, came out of the house with a shotgun aimed at the hostage's head. A police sniper shot the suspect in the heart. But before he died he fired on Corporal Hill and a fellow officer, killing Hill instantly. The wounded officer survived, yet sadly took his own life four years later due to the PTSD from which he suffered as a result of the incident.

Cpl. Charles William Hill

03/22/1989

Corporal Hill had been a New York City police officer before serving the city of Alexandria and its citizens for thirteen years. He left behind his wife and two sons. He had been one of my police academy instructors in 1982. Universally loved and respected by all of us in the class, he was the type of person who did all he possibly could to encourage our success. He was quick to smile and told more than a few war stories to his starry-eyed recruits.

* * *

Officer Philip Michael (Mike) Pennington of the Prince William County, Virginia, Police Department was killed on Thanksgiving Day, November 22, 1990. As a member of the SWAT team, Mike had responded to the residence of a suspect who earlier in the day had ambushed a captain of the Arlington County Sheriff's Department. Mike was the team's hostage negotiator. After determining that a forced entry was necessary to apprehend the suspect, who had been stalking police officers from a number of other jurisdictions, Mike and his fellow team members encountered the suspect with a pistol in hand. To evade capture, the suspect ran down the stairway to the basement. From the body bunker at the top of the stairs, Mike sought to talk the suspect into surrendering. Yet, unbeknown to Mike and the team, the suspect possessed an arsenal of weapons from which he suddenly produced a rifle and shot upward toward Mike. A bullet penetrated the body bunker as well as Mike's helmet, instantly killing him. As his fellow officers evacuated Mike from the residence, the suspect moved upstairs to resume the fight, at which point a SWAT team sniper and my former sergeant, Ben Fravel, shot and killed him.

Ofc. Phillip Michael Pennington

11/22/1999

Mike had just returned to the team after recovering from being shot earlier in the year during a drug incident. He left behind his wife and son. Five years later, his wife was sworn in as a Prince William County officer. Mike had served the citizens of Prince William County for eleven years prior to his death. He and I had worked on the same squad when I was with Prince William County. He wasn't the largest guy on the force, but he was a scrapper and a ball of energy. With a quick wit, he was respected and loved by his fellow officers and teammates.

* * *

Sgt. Robert Hienle

Shot 10/21/1998
Died 02/12/2010

Sergeant Robert Heinle of the Missoula City Police Department in Montana was shot on October 21, 1998. As a consequence of his wound, Bob was paralyzed from the neck down. He lived another eleven years before succumbing to complications related to his paralysis. Bob had been dispatched to a local bank to which a grifter had presented a forged check. Upon his arrival he engaged in a foot pursuit of the suspect who shot Bob in the neck. Convicted of attempted murder and other charges, the convict is serving a life sentence in prison. Bob left behind his wife who was one of the police dispatchers. He served the citizens of Missoula as an officer for seven years before the shooting, and was employed by the department for some time thereafter.

As a Missoula County sheriff's deputy, I responded to several calls with Bob, but my main contact with him was during the time we served together on the committee to build a local law enforcement memorial, commemorating the service of officers who had been injured or killed in the line of duty in Missoula County. In that endeavor we worked hand-in-hand with Lynette LePiane, the wife of our colleague, Sergeant Cliff LePiane, and the sister-in-law of fallen Officer Stephen LePiane. Ironically, Bob Heinle's name now adorns the memorial as a testament to him and to the hard work he undertook to bring it about as well as a deceased officer.

* * *

Attorney Judy Wang, an officer of the court and prosecutor for the city of Missoula, Montana, died September 25, 2009. Judy was by far the best prosecutor with whom I ever worked. She took the time to learn the cases that we presented to her. She was thorough in her work and fair to both officers and citizens. She sought our opinion before giving a break to persons whom she believed to be in need of a "hand up" rather than the clamping down of the heavy hand of justice. Yet she relentlessly prosecuted those whose crimes deserved incarceration.

Judy always took the time to prepare her officers for an upcoming trial. With me that was not always easy. She referred to me as being a bit impetuous when I got ahead of her during a trial. But she trusted my instincts even though she didn't always agree with my delivery. We lost only one trial simply because she couldn't convince a particular jury that driving impaired under the influence of alcohol did not mean that the driver had to be falling-down drunk. Among her other contributions, Judy Wang's name was synonymous with the domestic abuse laws of Montana and other states throughout the country. Having been not only a huge advocate for them, she became integrally involved in writing those laws for Montana.

City Attorney
Judy Wang Killed
09/25/2009

Judy ardently supported tough DUI laws and their enforcement, for which she was at times a crusader. Even though we stood at opposite ends of the political spectrum, I considered her a friend. She married one of my mentors, Carl Ibsen. They, too, had their political differences but worked them out. Their relationship was proof that opposites can attract and remain attached.

I received a heartbreaking call from Carl on the night of Judy's death, notifying me that she had been involved in a car accident on Interstate 90 near Deer Lodge, Montana. She had just taught a seminar on domestic abuse in Billings and was an hour and a half from home when a speeding drunk driver struck her from behind.

The tragic end to the life of a wonderful woman and twenty-five-year veteran prosecutor was a huge loss to the citizens of

Missoula, to the state of Montana, and to the country. She had been a driving force for justice, ironically killed by a drunk driver in spite of all of her efforts to get drunk drivers off of the road. As typically happens in such cases, the convicted driver got nowhere near the severity of sentence he deserved.

* * *

All of these persons were superb individuals who merited longer years on this earth than they had. They made many positive contributions to their departments, communities, and families. Their lives truly mattered.

Although the full extent of my own story has yet to be lived, I conclude with the words of the late General Douglas McArthur in his final address to Congress.

"Old soldiers never die, they just fade away," he said.

While we police officers also fade away, I should like to think that our honor, courage, commitment, and integrity live on in the hearts of the young lions who replace us.

EPILOGUE

I am now retired after a career spanning nearly thirty years. This time my retirement is likely to be for good. Yet who knows? Perhaps I will become a rookie again.

On second thought, I look forward to just being Papaw to my grandkids. They are a great blessing to us grandparents in our old age, for they represent the fulfillment of our hopes and dreams. They are the primary ones to whom we bequeath our human legacy, in the expectation that our best characteristics will be embodied in them long after our flesh and blood have returned to dust and ashes.

My life has been a blend of fortunate and unfortunate events, depending in part upon how they appear in hindsight. Looking back as I do, I can say without hesitation that, regardless of the failures and disappointments and surely for the triumphs and successes, I would not change anything. As for this present moment, I am exactly where I need to be, doing precisely what I enjoy doing.

Through my veins runs the blue blood of a police officer, covered by the redemptive blood shed by our Lord and Savior, Jesus Christ, as a result of which I am who I am, in both heart and spirit.

As a police officer, I have either arrested or issued citations to thousands of people over the years. I have answered thousands of calls in response to human crises. I hope and pray that none of those undertakings were in vain, but that I have served my fellow citizens as well as I possibly could.

It has been my honor and privilege to have worn the uniform and the badge of my profession and, above all, to serve alongside some of the greatest people I have ever known, who also wore the same badge and uniform. Together we have experienced many ups and downs, though mostly ups. Through the pain and sorrow, the happiness and joy of it all, I have been blessed to be a part of the Thin Blue Line.

My family has always supported me throughout the best as well as most challenging of circumstances. Because of the many hours of loving commitment that I devoted to my job, I missed out on a great deal of time with my family. My wife Carole has long lived with the knowledge that my work was my mistress. Yet she remained ever faithful to me, even when the pressures and dangers of any given day presented her with reason to fear what might happen to me, and consequently to her and our children. Carole turned toward me when a less loving wife may have turned against me. Clearly, she loved me with all of her heart. While she didn't always understand what I needed to do, or why I needed to do it, she nevertheless stood by my side. She was the rock upon whom I leaned, especially on those days and nights when unpredictable events shook the ground beneath me.

My kids, who today are my best friends, most certainly have loved me in spite of my parental deficiencies. Our grandkids naturally will know less of me and my vocation than do my children. Yet, from what my grandchildren learn from their parents, and not least from what they receive of me in the time I have remaining, as well as from this memoir, I hope they will come to appreciate the honorable value of the work I did and the badge I wore. If so, then I will have accomplished what I set out to do throughout my lifetime as the fruits of my labors accrue to their benefit. If they grow up to "back the Blue" in gratitude, and to respect the best of what cops everywhere stand for and do, then I will depart this life a happy man.

God has guided my footsteps every step of the way. It is God above all whom I thank for my wonderful journey through this life. As a man I am not rich, yet I am wealthy beyond measure when it comes to the love of my family and friends. And while I will never possess an earthly mansion, a heavenly one awaits me when my mortal days come to an end.

When I began this project, I figured that I would write but a few simple stories. That modest venture soon turned into a lengthy labor of love. The numerous memories that flooded the pathways of my mind were therapeutic for my soul as I pondered how each of them in some fashion had affected my life. Some of them had little impact, others caused me to smile, and still others dredged up old feelings and images that I thought I had buried years ago. Then, too, more than a few of them changed the course of my life. Taken together, they molded me into the person I am.

I trust that you, the reader, will have become better informed about what the general public commonly refers to, and yet only superficially knows, as police work. I trust, too, that you will have found some pleasurable entertainment among the people and events that lent humor and comic relief to me amid the dark and dangerous moments of this cop's life.

Most especially, I hope that when you see police officers walking their beat or stopping someone for a traffic offense, you will look upon those uniformed men and women for who they are as persons, and not simply for what they wear by way of dress or carry within their holsters. I hope that you will understand that we cops are your neighbors, your friends, and your family, but not your enemies. We have a difficult job to do, often under the most horrendous of circumstances. Yet we return to work day after day to protect the communities we love.

To my fellow officers in the line of duty, I hope that my story stirs your gratitude and aspiration, to remind you that you make a huge difference each day that you step out of your home to go to work on the streets and in the neighborhoods of our beloved land. You will not always see the fruits of your work firsthand. For the good that you do and the harm that you prevent by your very presence will seldom be more obvious to you than to those beneficiaries of your faithful actions.

As for those who fail to acknowledge your noble deeds, and yet are quick to point out your mistakes while overlooking their own misconceptions, do not lose heart. They are not the final judge of your labors. It is God's "well done, good and faithful servant" that matters most of all.

Wear your uniform and your badge with pride. As the symbols of your honor and the marks of your integrity, let them shine forth in brilliance and never sully the character and reputations of your brothers and sisters in Blue.

www.ingramcontent.com/pod-product-compliance
Lightning Source LLC
Chambersburg PA
CBHW070534170426
43200CB00011B/2424